Giron Escrima

Giron Escrima
Memories of a Bladed Warrior

Leo M. Giron
Grand Master Emeritus
Founder Bahala Na Martial Arts Association

EMPIRE Books
P.O. Box 491788, Los Angeles, CA 90049

Disclaimer
Please note that the author and publisher of this book are **NOT RESPONSIBLE** in any manner whatsoever for any injury that may result from practicing the techniques and/or following the instructions given within. Since the physical activities described herein may be too strenuous in nature for some readers to engage in safely, it is essential that a physician be consulted prior to training.

First published in 2006 by Empire Books
Copyright © 2006 by Empire Books
All rights reserved. No part of this publication may be reproduced or utilized in any form or by any means, electronic or mechanical, including photocopying, recording, or by any information storage and retrieval system, without prior written permission from Empire Books.

First edition
06 05 04 03 02 01 00 99 98 97 1 3 5 7 9 10 8 6 4 2
Printed in the United States of America.

Empire Books
P.O. Box 491788
Los Angeles, CA 90049

EDITED BY:
Antonio E. Somera
Grand Master Bahala Na Martial Arts Association
Little Manila Board Member
Legionarios Del Trabajo In America Member
Stockton Filipino American National Historical Society

EDITED BY AND PHOTOS BY:
James Sobredo, Ph.D.
Associate Professor
Department of Ethnic Studies
Asian American Studies Program
California State University, Sacramento

Library of Congress: 2006009385
ISBN-10: 1-933901-11-X
ISBN-13: 978-1-933901-11-4

Library of Congress Cataloging-in-Publication Data

Giron, Leo M., 1911-
  Giron escrima : memories of a bladed warrior / by Leo M. Giron. -- 1st ed.
    p. cm.
  Includes index.
  ISBN 1-933901-11-X (pbk. : alk. paper)
  1. Giron, Leo M., 1911- 2. Martial artists--Biography. 3. Escrima. 4. Martial arts--Philippines. 5. Hand-to-hand fighting, Oriental. I. Title.
  GV1113.G57A3 2006
  796.8092--dc22

2006009385

Dedication

I dedicate this book first to my beloved wife Alberta who inspired me and helped me to bring back memories of stories told when my mind was still alert and retentive. These are stories of fading experiences during World War II. She laughed when she heard my funny story about an old man squatting at attention saluting with his left hand with a big home made cigar in his mouth as we passed by. She laughed at the thought of me out speaking a Japanese cook in the guerrilla outfit in Japanese language simply because I was a little high on some homemade wine.

I also dedicate this book to my loyal assistant and good friend Tony Somera, who takes a high interest in the art, and who also encouraged me to write this book beginning with the first notes he took on a napkin at our favorite restaurant. I have given him the full responsibility as my heir to the art I founded, and the light of life that will guide him in the years to come, "Bahala Na."

I cannot summon enough knowledge and gather as many words to compose the feeling of gratitude for those that have helped me. I commend their inspiration to carry on the efforts of preserving and propagating the indigenous Filipino art of Escrima. My heartfelt thanks to all of them.

Leo M. Giron
Grand Master Emeritus
Founder Bahala Na Martial Arts Association

Acknowledgments

Acknowledgments for completion of this book are as follows in no particular order:
- Legionarios Del Trabajo In America
- Little Manila Foundation (Stockton)
- Filipino American National Historical Society
- Francisco Daguhoy Lodge #528
- Bahala Na Martial Arts Association
- Dr. & Master James Sobredo PHD
- Guro Kirk McCune, Bahala Na Martial Arts
- Empire Books—Mr. Jose Fraguas
- Grand Master Antonio & Mrs. Sally Flores Somera
- Mr. & Mrs. Chester S. Somera Sr.
- Escrima Coalition and Members
- Mr. & Mrs. Rob Farrens, In Shape City of California
- Guro Dan & Simo Paula Inosanto

Preface

I first met Grandmaster Leo M. Giron twelve years ago when I was completing my doctoral degree at UC Berkeley. He was an agile and amiable gentleman whose assuring voice and calm demeanor belied his martial arts expertise. Like many prospective students, I was interviewed by Grandmaster Giron, who asked about my background and my interest in the art, and he explained the uniqueness of the Giron Arnis Escrima system.

At that time, I had just married a local Stocktonian, starting a new family and commuting to a teaching job at Berkeley. Since Stockton was the home of Filipino martial arts, I decided to enroll in an escrima class. Seeing an advertisement in the local Filipino American newspaper, I called the Bahala Na Club's number, and Master Antonio "Tony" Somera answered the phone. Like Giron, Somera also spoke in an amiable pleasant manner and encouraged me to visit the Club where I ended up starting my lessons in escrima. Unfortunately, my doctoral studies and our move back to San Francisco interrupted my escrima studies.

Nearly ten years later, I returned to Stockton and was invited back to the Bahala Na Club by Tony Somera (now Grandmaster) to attend a graduation ceremony. By this time, old age had slowed Giron down, and he needed assistance in walking. I was glad that he still recognized me, but at the same time I was also saddened by his declining health. However, one thing stood out: Under the leadership of Grandmaster Somera, I noticed that the Club had grown to a fairly large membership, and there was a noticeably positive feeling among the members. What really surprised me, however, was Guro David Hines, a venerable gray-haired *white* guy, playing a crucial role in the graduation ceremony and reading to other mainly *white* escrimadors the duties and responsibilities of a Bahala Na escrima graduate. As a Filipino scholar, intellectual, and now practitioner of Bahala Na escrima, I actually see this direction as something positive. Observing the escrima ceremony, I know that these folks were white Americans, but in the process of practicing the Filipino art of escrima and pledging loyalty to the spirit and ideals of Giron's arnis-escrima, they were *culturally* Filipino. In a word, in my eyes, they had become Filipino. Today, as a practitioner of Bahala Na escrima, they are in fact my Filipino brothers.

The transition of the Grandmastership to Tony Somera signaled a major milestone in the Club's history. Giron's Bahala Na martial arts is now taught in member's clubs across the United States and at European clubs in England, Germany and Spain. Twice a year Bahala Na escrima practitioners come from all over the US and Europe to train in Stockton. In our Club one can hear instructions of the basic escrima drills in German and Castilian Spanish. Our racially/ethnically diverse members are Filipino, Chinese, Japanese, Korean, Mexican, African, Hawaiian, South American, German, English, and Spanish. Many of our members are also of mixed race parents.

Bahala Na is very unique among martial arts organizations because of their crucial role in bringing public awareness to escrima. For example, the story of Giron and Bahala Na martial arts has been incorporated as a regular part of a university class curriculum in California State University, Sacramento, where Somera's book and articles are used as part of a Filipino American class. Bahala Na members also accompany Somera and assist in classroom demonstrations. Somera has also delivered a lecture on Filipino American history and martial arts at the University of California-Davis. And each year students from UCLA and Stanford come and visit the Club to learn more about Filipino American martial arts and culture.

Bahala Na is also very unique because of their deep community activism and participation. Aside for performing public escrima demonstration for various community festivals—Barrio Fiesta and the Obon Festival—Bahala Na is deeply involved in the struggle to revitalize Stockton's Little Manila district. For instance, as a supporter of the Little Manila Foundation, the Bahala Na has raised thousands of dollars in support of redeveloping the downtown Stockton area, which has been designated as a historical district by the City of Stockton. Bahala Na members donned work clothes and helped in cleaning up and revitalizing downtown Stockton, especially the Iloilo Circle building, an event which brought out Mayor Edward Chavez and members of the press.

Finally, a shining moment occurred when Sergeant Leo M. Giron was interviewed by a PBS documentary crew in 2002. The interview occurred my house in Stockton, and that would be the last time that I spoke with the Grandmaster. Somera, who had a major role in Giron's film participation, helped the Grandmaster emeritus up the short steps to my house. When

Giron entered the house, right away the film crew knew they were in the presence of a very special person. In May 2005, PBS broadcasted nationally, on all their affiliate stations, "An Untold Triumph," a World War II documentary about Filipino American veterans and their important contributions to the US war effort in the Pacific. As one of the key figures in the documentary, Giron's story as a World War II commando was now being heard and broadcasted on national television.

Grandmaster Somera's leadership has brought a successful transition of Giron's legacy. It has also brought Bahala Na martial arts beyond the Stockton area and being just another Filipino martial arts organization. Somera has brought the Bahala Na martial arts to the next level. In the process Somera has maintained and remained true to the spirit of Leo M. Giron and the art of escrima.

James Sobredo, Ph.D.
Associate Professor
Department of Ethnic Studies
Asian American Studies Program
California State University, Sacramento

Foreword

It is a great honor for me to write the foreword on this story of my friend and teacher Grand Master Emeritus Leo M. Giron. He was a proud soldier who served our country with distinction and honor during World War II as a member of the 2nd Filipino Infantry. This story focuses on the true to life history of what that one man had to endure. As a sergeant in the United States Army, he was attached to General Douglas MacArthur's secret commando group the 978th signal outfit. His full name is Leovigildo Miguel Giron, a true Filipino American war hero.

During the outbreak of World War II Filipinos rushed to join the military to fight for their new found country, the United States of America, and to retake their homeland, the Philippine Islands. But because of a piece of racist legislation not allowing Filipinos to join the United States Army it would take a Presidential order to allow these Filipinos to join the military. The turnout of Filipinos to join the United States military was so great that the 1st Filipino Infantry would grow to the strength of nearly 12,000 men. This turnout was so overwhelming that the United States Army would need to form the 2nd Filipino Infantry a short time later. Out of these 12,000 men there would be less than 900 men who were selected as secret commandos to go behind enemy lines to become the eyes and ears for General Douglas MacArthur to make sure of his promise "I shall return." These men were dropped off by submarine nearly one year before any other American or Filipino American soldiers would land again on Philippine soil. These commandos went deep behind enemy lines and encountered the enemy in many hand-to-hand combat situations. Bahala Na, "come way may", was their slogan. These commandos were first trained in jungle warfare and were assigned to a camp called camp "X" in Australia. Their jungle training included the use of handguns, rifles, and lightweight radio equipment. They would learn Morse code, "wigwag" and the use of weather instruments all in the line of communications. But, as they reached the Philippine jungles, their specialty became hand-to-hand combat so as not to be detected by the enemy. Their mission was not to be noticed because this would give the enemy time to prepare for a United States invasion. Their weapon of choice was the bladed edged weapon called the bolo or "talonason." They spent many hours, days, and weeks learning the deadly martial art of their forefathers and ancestors.

They used their skills in the deepest parts of the Philippine jungles walking down many paths to reach their assigned destination with little or no apparent fear of encountering their enemies. They would travel from village to village to rid the native Filipinos of their warlord masters. This is the story of Sergeant Leovigildo Miguel Giron, told by him in his own words.

This book will also focus on Leo Giron in his role as Grand Master Emeritus. Nearly 20 years after World War II he introduced his system of Filipino Martial Arts called "Giron Arnis Escrima" and took the slogan of his World War II outfit "Bahala Na" to name his Filipino Martial Art Association. Giron taught his martial art to many thousands of students. Most importantly, along the way he also taught us his humble way of life. Many students pattern their own lives on these teachings even to this day. For me GME Giron taught me an art of life. Everything else was extra. This I will carry with me forever. I truly love "Uncle Leo" and I thank God that he allowed me to be a part of his life. He is my teacher and best friend.

To me Leo Giron is a true divine Martial Art Giant and World War II hero, a member of America's Greatest Generation.

Years before the passing of Grand Master Emeritus Giron he had instructed me to take his notes and manuscripts and put them into a book so that others could read his story and the history of the first generation of Filipinos that came to America with the dream of success and equality. His wish was to ensure that his words would be published into a book that represented the highest degree of honor, dignity and quality. Many years ago Grand Master and I met Mr. Jose Fraguas during a photo shoot in Los Angeles, California. Leo Giron was very impressed with Mr. Fraguas and his ability to publish books and magazines with the highest standards and with the degree of character for which Grand Master Emeritus himself was known. Mr. Fraguas and Grand Master Emeritus became instant friends and many times Mr. Fraguas would relate to Grand Master Emeritus as "Uncle Leo."

With my highest recommendation I can gladly say that this book will be a great addition to any martial artist's library and will also shine a light on

Grand Master Emeritus Leo M. Giron and Grand Master Antonio E. Somera of the Bahala Na Martial Arts Association.

the secrets of a battle proven Filipino Martial Art, and on the man who wrote this book. "Bahala Na"

    Antonio E. Somera
    Grand Master Bahala Na Filipino
    Martial Arts Association

Contents

Part 1: The Art of Escrima 1
   A History of Escrima 1
   1662 Rebellion and the Birth of Cabaroan 2
   Conditions Changed 3
   A New Concept of Escrima 4
   The Final Test 4
   The Scale of Justice 5
   The Final Crusade 6
   The Arrival of America 6
   The Champions 7
   The Art Migrated to America 8
   The Cultivation of Knowledge 9
   Discipline and Training 10

Part 2: World War II 13
   The Outbreak of War 13
   Premonition 15
   Requiem to My Masters 15
   Overseas 16
   The Final Test 16
   In Philippine Waters 17
   Intangible Power 18
   A Test of Stamina 19
   The Invasion of Lingayen Gulf 20
   Induction and Deduction 25
   At The Low Lands 34
   Thirty-Four Years Old 37
   AIB vs. CIC 38
   Jungle Freedom to Classical Military Life 40
   Home At Last 44
   Back to the Army Camp 46

Part 3: Civilian Life & Lessons from Escrima 49
Back to Civilian Life 49
Teaching Martial Arts Begun as a Hobby 50
Close Quarter Training 51
Escrima Lessons from a Bladed Warrior 52
    What Not To Do 52
    Justifiable Offense 53
    Rough Terrain 53
Lessons from War 54
Lessons from Life 55

Part 4: History of the Filipino Lodge 59
History of the Legionarios del Trabajo 62
Francisco Daguhoy 72
Daguhoy Filipino Lodge 73
Daguhoy Filipino Museum 76

Part 5: History of Escrima in Stockton 81
Early History of Escrima in America 81
History of Escrima in Stockton 82

Part 6: Last of the Bladed Warriors 93

Part 7: Twenty Styles of Grand Master Leo M. Giron 103

Lineage of Giron Arnis Escrima
Bahala Na Martial Arts Association 304

Part 1
The Art of Escrima

A History of Escrima

Many writers of martial art books and short articles pertaining to the combat art of escrima borrow information from others who might have claimed high honors and holding high degrees in contest arenas. These articles or books are glamorized with beautiful words that blend so well into the text and are designed to make the picture seem so realistic and captivating. This approach certainly glorifies the martial arts hero of the story to the highest degree, bringing him fame, and in many cases makes the reader believe that the art is distinctive and unique. One is made to believe that no other similar escrima style exists and no place familiar with their style of martial arts.

My goal in writing this book is to gradually shape the mind of the reader in the direction of the Filipino art of escrima. Escrima is a Filipino art. No other nationality ever used this style self-defense prior to its exposure during the 400 years of fierce battles with the Spaniards. There were no firearms during those periods other than a few single shot muskets used by the Spaniards. Those who fought against the Spaniards fought well, and, with their single-edged bolos, they defeated their better-equipped opponents in battle. However, eventually, the Spaniards with their metal breastplates, iron armor, and modern large steel swords and muskets were a match for the skilled and fierce Filipino warriors they battled, and the Philippines were colonized by the Spaniards.

I am native son of the town of Bayambang in the Province of Pangasinan in Northern Philippines. I begin my story with the 1662 Rebellion against the

Spaniards by King Andres Malong. Malong's kingdom was in the barrio of Binalatongan in the town of San Carlos in Pangasinan Province. San Carlos is approximately one hour from Bayambang by horse or 15 minutes by automobile.

The 1662 Rebellion is the focal point of my writing because that is where the "new style" of escrima was born—what is called *Cabaroan* in Ilocano (fig. 1). It was during this time of struggle against the Spanish regime that the new concepts of escrima *(cabaroan)* was born and would eventually evolve and became as they are known and practiced today. I will tell the story of the 1662 Rebellion of as closely and as accurately as it was told to me after being handed down through the generations.

Fig. 1—GME Giron with his cabaroan weapon.

Fig. 2—GME Giron with his 24 inch bolo knife.

1662 Rebellion and the Birth of Cabaroan

The army of King Malong was made up of warriors who were experts in the art of escrima. They were skilled practitioners of *cadaanan*, the "old style" of escrima, which is distinguished by the use of a shorter bolo blade. These Filipinos were fast with the bolo and had a wealth of experience in tournaments and military combat. Furthermore, it was said that most had the battle scars from actual combat. These Filipinos carried short bolos blade that were anywhere from 18 to 24 inches in length (fig. 2).

The Spaniards were cruel and disrespectful to the native Filipinos and were never concerned about their lives and welfare. With military support, the Spanish government was taking unfair advantage of the Filipino people. These conditions of oppression led King Malong to prepare an army for battle against the Spaniards.

Neighboring provinces in Pangasinan provided both men and military supplies. During the rebellion, the Spaniards forced other Filipinos to fight against Malong and against other Filipinos. Very few Spaniards, only those that were in immediate command, were in the battlefields. Malong was unable to recruit Filipinos for reinforcements or obtain allies as the Spaniards had succeeded in blocking all incoming trails to his headquarters. Eventually, after a couple of years of fighting, Malong's army was crushed, and many any of Malong's rebels surrendered but most died in battle. The remaining army took to the hills, and, out of pride, these patriots refused to surrender. In the hills, as supplies ran low, conditions worsened. Many of the rebels became restless, and drinking became common, but even that was short-lived, as the supply of liquor eventually ran out.

Conditions Changed

The native Filipinos of the surrounding barrios were providing support and supplies for Malong's rebels. The natives eventually became tired of volunteering their food and supplies. As a result, the rebels began to rob the neighboring barrios. In some cases, the so-called "patriots" were even raping young women of the barrios and killing those Filipinos who resisted. They had become *bandidos*, bandits. As more barrios were raided by the rogue rebels, the sufferings of the native Filipino population increased, and yet the Spanish regime continued a hands-off policy as long as Spaniards were not directly affected. As the years went by, the young boys of the barrios grew into manhood. These young barrio men had witnessed the many misfortunes of their family and friends. In many cases, they themselves were victims of atrocities at the ages of five or six and now, at sixteen and seventeen, they were old enough to fight back.

These young barrio men were taught escrima by the veterans of Malong's army who had surrendered, lived and worked with the barrio folk, and avoided succumbing to a life of banditry that befell their former compatriots who were hiding in the hills. The barrio veterans taught these boys how to fight with longer weapons. The veterans used a blade, about 20 inches long, attached to a handle of approximately the same length. These knives were called *panabas* and were made for the purpose of chopping down bushes and small trees in order to clear virgin soil for farming (fig. 3).

The reason for the extra long handle is to provide enough distance between the protruding branches and the hands. Chopping is more effective due to the fact that the weight of the *panabas* is at the upper half or end of the instrument.

Fig. 3—GME Giron striking GM Somera right arm with his 42 inch Panabas.

A New Concept of Escrima

Eventually this younger generation of barrio young men began to teach their comrades this new and exciting style of escrima. A year passed since their training, and it was also about the time that the hill raiders would be making their annual visit. Consequently the barrio defenders' training became much more intense. They practiced during moonlit nights or with light provided by primitive lanterns and torches. A sentry was always placed at the far end of the trail to provide a warning in the event that unfamiliar intruders came by. The young men became confident that their new style would out do the *bandidos*. Soon these young warriors would meet the veterans. The new would test the old.

The Final Test

The long-awaited hour finally arrived, and the battle was about to begin. There was mixed emotions among the young men. Some were calmer and confident while others were eager and chattering. Their teachers hushed them saying, "*Calma, calma…distancia mas distancia.*"

The barrio boys were dispersed behind coconut trunks and bushes, while the reserves hid under houses. As the raiders entered the village, the dogs barked furiously sensing the dangerous nature of these men. The *bandidos'* commanders were on horse back while the rest entered on foot. In the meantime, the audible command tingled into the ears of young barrio defenders, "*Flataque, ataque, distancia!*" Bolos were drawn and steel met steel with sparks filling the air. Men clashed, screamed, and some slumped with their final cry. Some screamed, "*Retira, retira!*" The gaps between combatants closed. Every possible route of escape was guarded. In one hour the screaming of women and children subsided. The barrio mothers ran in frenzy to see if their young warriors—their sons—were safe. Some had minor injuries, while a few were more seriously hurt. All in all the barrio defenders were victorious. The old men and women led the burial detail, and the young ladies provided food, while the warriors checked their weapons, honed and repaired some of the chips, and washed away the blood stains.

The Scale of Justice

The Spanish authorities came down to find out what had occurred and were pleased to see that the *bandidos* who had created so many disturbances in practically all the villages were eliminated. The *bandidos* were the remnants of Malong's revolutionary forces, so their defeat provided good reason for Spanish approval. A few of the ranking officers were amazed with the long *panabas* that were used to defeat the former patriots. The commandante measured, "*Quarinta polgadas, quatro pies. Muy bien. Mano largo esta bien.*"

The year went by and peace prevailed, but the new style of fighting continued to be used. It was now called *Larga Mano* (fig. 4), the simplified and safe new style.

Fig. 4—GME Giron striking GM Somera right hand playing the larga mano style.

News traveled fast and the neighboring provinces heard about it. The ban on escrima that had been put into effect long ago was never lifted, but the authorities were reluctant to put pressure on the villagers to stop since the victory over the former Malong rebels brought praise to the local authorities from provincial and local governments.

The Final Crusade

The years went by and the hardship that was common under military rule persisted. The final fight for Filipino freedom took place in the year 1896. Jose Rizal, a Chinese mestizo and an expert in fencing, planted the seeds of dissent among Filipinos when he published his novels *Noli Me Tangere* and *El Filibusterismo*, novels heavily critical of the Spanish government. An educated scholar (*ilustrado*) and physician, Rizal wrote about the Spanish government's bad treatment of Filipinos and pushed for reforms in the colonial government. Rizal, however, did not start the armed struggle for independence.

Andres Bonifacio was born in a humble home in Tondo, Manila, attended school in Cebu, would become a clerk in a rattan company, and many Filipinos consider him to be Father of Filipino Nationalism. Bonifacio formed a secret organization called *Kataastaasan Kagalanggalang Katipunan*.

Emilio Aquinaldo, another mestizo *ilustrado*, would replace Bonifacio to become the President of the First Philippine Republic. Aguinaldo declared Philippine independence in Kawit, Cavite in June 12, 1898. The Philippine Republic would last for only a few months. The Filipino struggle for independence against the Spanish would come to a stalemate and the leadership of the Katipunan would leave the Philippines, regroup, and later return to continue their fight for independence. This time the Katipunan will be fighting against the United States of America.

The Arrival of America

In 1898 the Americans led by Admiral George Dewey fought the Spanish Navy in Manila Bay, crushing the Spanish fleet. After several years of fighting with the Spanish, the Filipinos were again forced to fight to keep their flag of freedom waving. The Veteranos de la Revolucion and Defensores de la Libertad were pressed into battle once more. These weak militias were low on supplies and manpower but nevertheless, fought ferociously.

The Americans proved to be better rulers for they were kind to the people. Immediately, schools were built and children were encouraged to be educated. In no time the youngsters were speaking English.

The escrimadores presented their arts to these new American governors, assuring them that it was effective against the Castillans. The Americans quickly won the friendship of the people because they were more liberal. They looked into the difficulties of the people and endeavored to improve conditions when it was possible. By now, the veterans did not fear the sight of the white man. It was no longer necessary to summon the rest of the villagers to draw their bolos and throw themselves into a skirmish with the cry, "Anak ng bukid sumilang kayo" (arise, sons of the mountains). This time the art of escrima was no longer banned since the Americans carried the Enfield rifle and escrima cannot defeat firearms. Escrima became one of the many sports in the Philippines—sipa and cock fighting being the most popular, while escrima was secondary. At the time there were no gear to protect against injuries, which is why only the best escrimadores went into the arena for national competitions. Women also competed in local contests.

The Champions

The new stars of the art demonstrated their prowess under the limelights. The arena in the city of Dagupan, Pangasinan, was the most common place to prove oneself. These fights took place immediately after World War I. Santiago Toledo was the star outshining all other competitors of the time. Toledo was a native of the town of Binalonan, Pangasinan, but because of his reputation and popularity he was forced to reside in Dagupan to be immediately available when and if there was a challenge. Escrima competitions took place every day of the week except Sunday, which was the day that was reserved for cock fighting. Toledo was not only the champion. He was also the big maestro.

There were other champions in neighboring communities, but they were not able to beat Toledo. There was a good practitioner by the name of Francisco Garcia from the nearby town of Calasiao in Pangasinan Province. There was also a young contender by the name of Juan Gombay from the town of Bani. Many old Filipinos believed that Toledo was invincible. They believed that he was endowed with supernatural powers, because he could stretch farther than any of his challengers and contemporaries. They said that he had the stretching ability of an earthworm or a night crawler. It was thought that he may have befriended the Prince of these creatures and out of merit he earned his unusual ability. Many Filipinos believe in *anting-antings*, which are amulets and charms providing protection. Many believed that Toledo remained a champion because of this reputation. No one wanted to fight this idol. An escrimador fighting for the crown needed to firmly set his mind into believing that he would not be injured, that he would win, and that for him, there was no such thing as *anting-anting*. "Bahala Na," "Come what may," must be his slogan.

As the years passed and Toledo was beyond his prime, a young man named Dalmacio Bergonia was born in the neighboring province of La Union. He emerged in the seaport of Aparri, Cagayan Province. Although this lad was born in a western town, due to the profession of his father, he grew up in the northeastern corner of Luzon. His father owned a sea-faring *banka*, a sailboat that transported cargoes by sea from one port to another. Because Bergonia had to go to school like the rest of the children, he was forced to stay ashore. At times, however, Bergonia would go aboard the *banka* with his father, and he met a lot of men with different abilities in martial arts. A few of them were residents of the town of Aparri. Now a growing lad, Bergonia took interest in the art of escrima. While in public school, he was teased about the black and blue marks that he had received when he was unable to ward off oncoming blows. But these marks did not bother him; he claimed that he did not feel the impact, that the blows did not hurt him. The strong blows delivered by an adult should have been sufficient to disable and maim him, but the growing boy was impervious to their strikes. No bones were broken.

Eventually, word got out that Bergonia had inherited from his grandfather an *anting-anting*. People believed that he had the nature of a dried coconut husk since with the exception of a bladed weapon no Filipino weapon could hurt him. The stick would bounce off him and leave him unharmed. Dalmacio had many years of experience and had developed several styles due to his acquaintances with those of various skills and techniques. At the height of his strength and skill, Delmacio took the crown. There was no age restriction on fighters for the title at that time.

At this time many young Filipinos were recruited to work at the sugar plantation in Hawaii. Most of Dalmacio's contemporaries were enticed into traveling to America and the land of opportunity. Bergonia, however, remained and continued to teach escrima in Aparri. He became famous for a fad among a few escrimadores known as the double stick style, which was called the *Macabebe* style.

The Art Migrated to America

Several of Bergonia's contemporaries met other experts in Hawaii, many of whom came from different parts of the Philippines. One expert, one of the few graduate students of Bergonia, also migrated to Hawaii. His name was Flaviano Vergara, who hailed from the town of Santa Cruz, in the

Province of Ilocos Sur. Flaviano also lived the life of a sea-faring man. He served in a *banka* as a chief and one of his responsibilities was to determine how many sails were to be hoisted in order to outrun the other *bankas*, thus getting to the nearest and best docks in port. Side-swiping a boat often resulted in serious fights, and Flaviano was familiar with these experiences. While in Hawaii, Flaviano, a quiet and well-mannered man, had several escrima encounters that tested his skill, speed, and courage. It has been said that Flaviano was never hit.

The Cultivation of Knowledge

I had the rare opportunity of working with Vergara Flaviano in a prune orchard in 1929. This was in the little town of Meridian west of Yuba City, California. I was the bookkeeper in the farm during harvest season, and as the season progressed Flaviano took interest in imparting to me some of his knowledge in self defense. We played far away from the camp, since Flaviano would not teach in the presence of another person. He was very careful to see that no one should acquire his rare knowledge and represent it in a way that might discredit him. Flaviano despised braggarts and disapproved of impatience. His slogan was, "There's a time for everything." He preferred not to be known as an expert escrimador; consequently, he was able to enjoy the serenity of a peaceful life without wondering when and where a challenge would arrive.

Once Flaviano raised his eyebrows and confided in me the following story.

"Young man," he explained to me, "not because I myself is telling you instead of another, but the way I figure and the way I feel, I think the challenger that will beat me is not yet born."

As my training went on, he detected that my movement demonstrated some knowledge in the art.

He modestly queried, "Will you honestly tell me if you have had any training from any teacher before?"

I was being tested not only in my knowledge of escrima, but in my honesty and full confidence of my teacher.

"Benito Junio, Julian Bundoc, Fructuso Junio," I explained. "I doubt if you know them!"

"No, I don't know them," Flaviano retorted.

"Yes," I replied. "*Them.*"

My first instructor Benito Junio was a drunkard but a very good fighter nonetheless. Then there was my cousin Julian Bundoc, who graduated from the same teacher. Then there was a man named Fructuso Junio who drew the line between the *cabaroan* (new) and *cadaanan* (old).

"Is that all?" Flaviano asked.

I nodded my head.

In a very low voice he sighed, "At least you are honest."

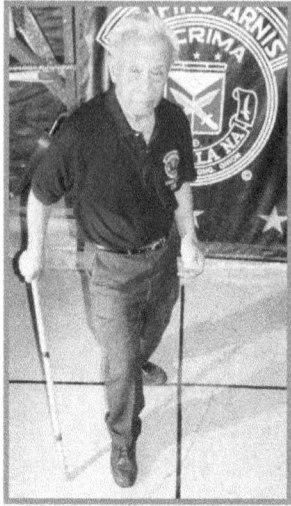

Fig. 5—GME Giron also very critical of foot position.

Discipline and Training

Flaviano was very critical of how I placed my feet (fig. 5). An over indulgent and aggressive right hand fighter can, if he lacks control, cut his own leg if he persists in placing his left foot forward. Most especially when the delivery comes down from the upper right. His first set of instructions were: a right handed fighter should endeavor to place his right foot forward at all times.

"There may be a few exceptions," Flaviano said. "But experience tells me that it is safer and more important that your reaching not be impaired." Left hand practitioners should follow the reverse.

Vergera's second instruction was, "Never be too eager to win a bout before you are certain what style your opponent will launch against you."

"It pays to have the knowledge of more than one style," he continued. "So that you can choose the one that is the most appropriate without jeopardizing your safety."

Flaviano explained that the fighter should have the knowledge of two distinct styles: the old and the new, the close quarter combat and the distant and safe style.

"I advocate the quiet type of escrimador," he explained in his third set of instructions. "Do you know why? Let me tell you. If you have a loose mouth so that your tongue does not stop waggling, the time will come when you will be over-indulgent and brag about what you know.

"You will try continually to make others believe that you are really good and that you were never defeated in the arena. True or false, one day there will be someone who will have the courage to respond to your incessant challenges.

"You will be force to stand behind your exuberance. Since you made all the noises you will have to be the aggressor, and this is the exact opposite of the principle that I put forth.

"I would rather be challenged and play the part of a defender and apply the waiting technique. Every man has the urge and strong desire to be famous; many will stop at nothing to pursue this inclination to be well known. However, one must be well disciplined, and one must realize the fact that learning escrima is purely for *self-defense*.

"I did not offer to teach you so that you would become an aggressor. That is why my method of teaching limits you to no more than your own defense. Your trainer will strike and if you do not defend yourself you will get hurt. You do not counter-strike but you may simulate this. This is the difference between this style, *De Fondo* (fig. 6), which is your base, and the *Larga Mano* (fig. 7), which is the opposite extreme.

"Some will say your *De Fondo* is boring for it is not fluid. Certainly, it is patterned for that purpose. It is up to the student after graduation to continually conceive of ways to fill the gaps, the space between the two extremes."

Years went by and each of us followed the harvest season to different farm communities. Flaviano did not come back to Meridian or any other fruit orchard I worked in. I remained in Yuba and Sutter counties working in the peach, plum, and prune orchards. The thought of escrima rarely came to my mind, and in fact it was beginning to fade away. The knowledge remained but the lack of another enthusiast to spar with allowed the art to become merely imbedded in the self.

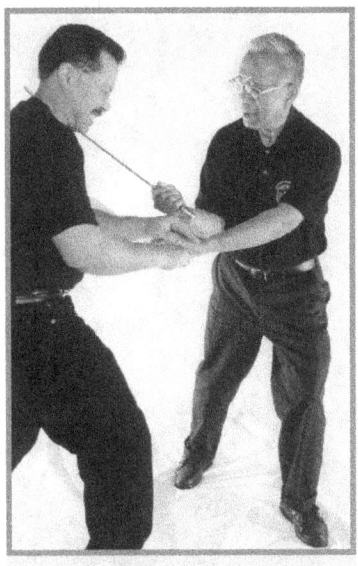

Fig. 6—GME Giron striking the throat of Somera playing the de fondo style.

Fig. 7—GME Giron striking the left shoulder of Somera playing the larga mano style.

Part 2
World War II

The Outbreak of War

Twelve years later after I met Flaviano in America, on December 7th, 1942, the Japanese bombed Pearl Harbor and Manila in a surprise attack. Practically every Filipino was inducted into the army (fig. 1). I was a farmer in Imperial Valley at the time and was considered essential on the home front. Eventually, in October of 1942, I was permitted to join the service. I was first stationed at Camp San Luis Obispo, and then in the winter of the same year I was transferred to Fort Ord. Prior to Thanksgiving, I encountered a man appearing to be a new recruit walking near the local theater. I looked twice because of the Toscani cigar I saw in his mouth and the shabby sort of walk that I thought I recognized.

Flaviano, I said to myself.

It's got to be him. No one else walks that way. Because of his rigid training in escrima, both feet pointed in opposite directions to facilitate the shifting of the weight of the body to either side. When we recognized each other our faces gladdened. He had been inducted two weeks earlier to Regimental Headquarters and I was stationed with company G annex.

The following weekend every soldier was given passes to Salinas to see their girl friends or relatives. Everyone hated to stay at the base for there was nothing to see but GIs. Flaviano visited the barracks, and we talked about the past. He asked if I still remembered what he had taught me. It had been a long time since the two of us had worked together. We cut a couple of old broom handles and we worked out between the bunks. It didn't take long for me to pick up some of the things that were a bit rusty. More swinging and a little

Fig. 1—First Filipino Infantry at Hunter Leggett Military Reservation.

training was added every night. During weekdays, after dinner when everyone changed into their class "C" uniform and met in the rec hall or the PX, Flaviano and I trained in escrima. Between drills we would talk. Sometimes a soldier would come back to the bunks and ask what we were doing. Some would tell us that they would never come close to a Samurai sword. They claimed they would give the Samurai bearer a load of their M-1.

Weeks went by and Flaviano and I did nothing but drill and drill. On the afternoon of Christmas Eve, I received my first stripe and I rushed to sew it on my uniform. I received the highest score on the .22 caliber range. Flaviano and I went to the recreation hall to show off my first stripe. I sort of walked side ways to show off the stripe. Someone jested, "Hey, hey. Look at the general. He earned his first turkey wishbone. You'll go to work now."

Premonition

The year was close to its end. As our discussions of various subjects progressed, Flaviano said with sincerity, "I'm glad that you took interest in learning the art because at least you have something to remember me by.

"I have a feeling," he said as he placed his hand on his chest, "that I am not going to come out of this war."

I told him that he was crazy. He assured me that when he had this feeling in the past he was able to alter his plans and avert what he suspected what was going to happen. He claimed that this had always worked, but this time, since he was in the service, he would have to change their plans and this was not possible.

Flaviano said to me, "Now you listen to me very carefully. Like I told you, your training is the only memento of our friendship, and I want you to treasure it.

"Do you remember," he continued, "what I told you about the two extremes of your art? The base is the *De Fondo*, a close quarter combat style while the *Larga Mano* uses distance and is the safer of the two. You must be very happy that you have the two because you can tell the difference between the old and the new."

I nodded my head intently and he said to me, "Suppose someone presented to you a style totally strange to you. You do not recognize it as the old or the new. What are you going to do?"

"Is there such a thing," I asked, as my curiosity was peaking. "Are there anymore?"

He smiled and took a piece of my writing paper and folded it to make it into a crude-looking fan. Pointing at the left end he said, "This is your old style." He then pointed to the right side and said, "This is your new style. How about these in the middle? These are the unexpected, and this is why a master must be able to fill these gaps. These are the "master's secrets" and I entrust them to you. I have held them from you for many years but now they are yours as a remembrance of me.

Requiem to My Masters

The year ended and on January 2nd, my Regiment moved to Camp Cooke and Flaviano's moved to Camp Beale. I never saw him again. I heard when I was in Milne Bay, New Guinea that Flaviano's outfit was in Oro Bay, which was on the other side of New Guinea. Before I was shipped to the Philippines from Australia, on August 18, 1944, I learned that Flaviano was killed in a dynamite explosion. It was not a Japanese bullet that killed him.

It was dynamite. I never found out the exact details of how and why this happened. My friend was gone. My Master gave me his most valuable treasure: The secret knowledge of a master in the art of escrima.

Overseas

I was shipped out of New Guinea to Australia on January 10, 1944, to a place called Camp X. It was close to the little town of Beau Desert and about 60 miles from the seaport of Brisbane in Queensland. It was here that I furthered my training in Morse code, cryptography, visual communication, and other methods of communication. I also embarked on my final training in jungle warfare in a place called Canungra. Thirteen weeks of hard training contributed to my ability in climbing the high mountains of the Philippines. At this point I was a Staff Sergeant.

On August 10, 1944 I was ordered to a briefing at the General's Headquarters. General Douglas MacArthur wore five gold stars and crossed his arms when he spoke.

"Boys," he said. "I selected you to do a job that a General can't do. You have the training to do a job that no one else can do. You are going home to our country, the Philippines. Yours and my homeland. You will serve as my eyes, my ears, and my fingers, and you'll keep me informed of what the Japanese are doing.

"You will tell me how to win this war by furnishing me with this information which I could not obtain in any other way. Good luck, and there will be shining bars waiting for you in Manila."

The Final Test

At dawn on August 12, 1944, we waved farewell to the General and the rest of the military big shots and in the evening we were in Fort Darwin. The submarine USS Sting Ray was waiting for us, and the sailors looked at us incredulously and said, "Is it really that bad?"

We were armed to the teeth. We had carbines, submachine guns, side arms of .45 caliber Colt automatics, bolo knives, trench knives, brass knuckles, and .38 caliber silencers. Our ammunition was loaded ahead of us in special packages.

While enroute to the Philippines, we slept on our own cargo boxes. One other soldier and I slept under the torpedo racks. One night the sub was rumbling a bit more than usual, so I asked one of the sailors what was going on. He told me that the sub had been fired upon and had to out maneuver the torpedoes at full speed. This occurred near the Halmahera Island on the Celebes Sea.

In Philippine Waters

The sub traveled around the eastern and western side of Luzon while looking for a good landing area. Captain Loomis suggested that we disembark at Daluperi Island, one of the many islands in the Batanes group, about 20 miles north of Luzon. We had reports that there were about 10,000 Japanese on the island so we politely told the captain to drop us anywhere in Luzon as long as it had Philippine soil.

On August 28th, they found a little beach on the northern tip of Luzon, took some scouting pictures of the area and then decided to land there. It was Caonayan Bay, and during that night we left the sub and made our way to it. The sub was forced to wait for nightfall at a depth of 210 feet. We had been spotted by radar and a plane was dropping depth charges on us. They came close enough to rattle the sub and burst some pipes but luckily this was the extent of the damage. By nightfall the Japanese planes gave up but we still had some difficulties to contend with. There were problems due to the passing of a large Japanese convoy bringing troops and supplies to Leyte where the Americans had landed 8 days earlier. A little rubber boat that carried a few of our supplies and propaganda equipment had a hard time going over and through the giant waves that the big ships created. Two rubber boats full of cargo went ashore while 10 men stayed in the sub. The lieutenant and myself and three other men went ahead on trial boats and only two of the 15 tons of cargo were unloaded. It was getting too hot and Captain Loomis said via the walkie-talkie that the sub had to leave. He told me that they would wait if we wanted to turn back.

"We are in our homeland now," I said. "No thank you. We will stay."

I'm cutting out many of the details in the complicated landing but there is one more story to tell. At the mouth of the river that emptied into the sea was a house that had been seized by a Japanese patrol which had been retrieving floating cargo from a Japanese boat that had been sunk by a British submarine the day before. A detachment of about 2 squads patrolled the beach on this moonlit night. We had 2 tons of cargo hidden behind green bushes above the beach where also we sought to hide.

As the head of the Japanese column entered the village we occupied, 15 submachine guns opened fire. Fifteen Japanese were hit and the rest escaped. A few of us were forced to take out our bolo knives and make sure no one was left to tell who had attacked them. Civilians came to help dig shallow graves on the beach and an old man harnessed his carabao to drag a dried limb of a tree to erase our tracks on the beach.

The following afternoon, a couple of waves of Japanese soldiers entered the barrio. Some of the civilians were beaten and asked about the attack on the Japanese soldiers. They answered that it was guerrillas that had attacked. We watched this through binoculars on a knoll overlooking the village. The civilians were smart not to reveal the landing of American commandos.

The slogan of our battalion was *Bahala Na* ('Come what may!'), which suggested that we were brave, but in reality we were all scared. Our first initiation in blood made us feel guilty and remorseful. We had seen war in the movies but it was a lot different when we were in it ourselves.

Intangible Power

We left the beach on August 29th, and I was introduced to anting-anting, the supernatural power I had always heard about.

Old man Pablo, one of the senior villagers was asked by the barrio chief to go ahead and perform his special rituals. His instructions to us were to follow him, keep absolutely quite, and not to mind anything we saw on the trail. "Do not look around," he said. In order not to break loose from the column, we were told to grab a handful of luminous mushrooms growing between the rotten leaves. We held it behind our backs so the man behind us could see and keep pace with us. We went through a swamp with water about a foot deep and we could see pairs of eyes when we turned on our flashlights. They were crocodiles, the nearest to the trail was about 5 feet long and the largest was around 6 feet. We passed through the swamp and barrio. With as many houses and dogs that there were, one would think that the entire neighborhood would have been alarmed and awakened. The Japanese headquarters was at the second house on the trail entering the village.

Old man Pablo stood by the side, let us by and said in our dialect, "Keep on and don't look back." The old man had an almost burned out candle still lit which we were informed later was used in the ritual. How did he hide our presence to the dogs, geese, and ducks that were in the village? What power accomplished this? Their barrio chief that came up to show us where to hide told us Pablo could always be relied upon in tight situations.

We penetrated deeper into the jungle to a higher elevation. This was necessary first to avoid Japanese patrols and get better radio reception, and second, to have access to other non-Christian natives. With them, we could barter for sweet potatoes with our extra GI shirts. Money was unimportant to them since they rarely got into town.

A Test of Stamina

On August 29th, we left the beach. The boys from the village and the barrio chief transported our 2 tons of cargo a portion at a time each night to our hiding place. Our radio communications were going well, and two months later on October 12th, we were contacted by our agent, a member of the Philippine guerilla forces. We were told that the 15th Infantry Regiment Philippine Army was on its way to clean out spies in the northern communities. Our agents made contact with their commanders, so they would forego the mission of cleaning out the spies and collaborators. Instead they escorted us to the General Headquarters of Northern Luzon. On October 13th, we followed the United States Armed Forces in the Far East (USAFFE) trail and three days later arrived in the town of Manabo, in the Province of Abra. The 15th Infantry Philippine Army commanded by Captain John O'Day could not go beyond Manabo, because this was the sector controlled by the 121st Infantry Regiment commanded by Major Barnett.

Before we got to Manabo we stopped in several communities. We traveled through the towns of Peddig, Dingras Ilocos Norte, and also Banna where we found two spies, a man and a woman. We knew that the man was a spy because he was wearing a brand new silk shirt and in time of war no one could afford to buy such an item. They arrested him right away and found a little booklet, which identified him as a *UN* (United Nippong). He was shot on the spot.

In each town that we visited, we were fed and the town celebrated our arrival. At one particular town, I remember that after the town meeting, a beautiful young girl was asked to sing for us. Before her song, she said, "I wish my two brothers could be here in this struggle, but it was their misfortune to have died in Bataan." She wiped her tears and added, "As soon as I learned that the US landing forces were moving south, I did not hesitate to come meet these brave heroes from the USA." She then proceeded to sing a beautiful song. She was superb.

We broke up for the afternoon to take a rest. On the way to the headquarters, I got suspicious and asked Captain O'Day how the beautiful girl knew that we were US soldiers, and how did she know we were moving south. Captain O'Day spit his chewing tobacco and said, "Son of a bitch, she must be a spy. No one is suppose to know all of this information." The young girl was arrested and during the investigation, she broke down and confessed and surrendered her booklet, another UN book. Captain O'Day was superstitious about executing women, so instead of executing her, she was put in the custody of L Company and put to work in the laundry department.

We went on through the towns of La Paz and then Dolores where the Woman's Auxiliary service treated my feet because of fungus that was growing on the soles. We then continued, went on crossing rivers and hiking and, after a few days, my feet were raw and ready to bleed. We traveled to the town of San Juan where I was forced to dance their native dance called Tadek, which had the rhythm provided by a couple of symbols. It was quite a sight, this dance of mine. Everyone present nearly died laughing. We continued, and it took us 37 days to reach our destination.

On Christmas Eve 1944, I was sent with a squad of experienced riflemen to meet a submarine loaded with arms, ammunition, and medical supplies. The submarine *USS Norwalk* was to rendezvous with us at Darigayos, La Union, but there were problems since the 2,000 civilians who were to unload the cargo were chased off by Japanese soldiers. The submarine moved to a secondary sight in San Esteban, Ilocos Sur. My men and I had to return as soon as it became dark, while men from the Eastern and Central sectors unloaded the submarine. Most of our work, for a while, was routine reconnaissance and communications.

The Invasion of Lingayen Gulf

On January 9th thru the 12th, 1945, we were in full combat. Leyte had already been taken, and at early dawn on the 9th the first salvo of the biggest US Navy guns buzzed over our heads. The target was Baguio and they were shooting from the sea. We happened to be between these two points. Baguio was full of Japanese soldiers; however, four days of bombing and the landing of troops in Lingayen Gulf gave the Japanese plenty to deal with. Many Japanese soldiers and labor battalions roamed about in large groups, many of them were bandaged or on crutches without any notion of where they should go for help. They were not armed and surrendered willingly. We had no cages or compounds for them, and we were short of food and could not feed them. We were planning a victory party but the celebration would be short lived for me.

On January 13th, Major Maglaya showed me a radiogram that said, "Technical Sergeant, Leovigildo Giron will proceed to Highway 5, 5th military district, and join the 14th Infantry Regiment, commander, Major Romulo Manriquez, to assist in restoring radio communication. By order of General Krueger, Philippine attack force commander."

After reading this I wilted. I was ordered to go alone. Tears rolled down my cheek as I asked Major Maglaya, "Why me, and alone at that?" All he could say was, "I'm sorry my friend, but you have the brains and the know-how. You were selected; you should be proud."

I packed my gear, my radio transceiver, generator, carbine, submachine gun, and 6 extra loaded clips of .45 caliber ammunition for my M-3 submachine gun—six clips at 30 rounds, not counting the clip already in the machine gun, weighed quite a bit. My shoes were resoled for me in record time. I had eight native Filipino *cargadores* assigned to assist me carry gear, none of whom could speak English fluently, so we had a hard time communicating in very simple English. We loaded up our gear and set off on our trek. The afternoon of the 13th, with only one of them speaking very little English, we all met for a briefing. I told them that at 3:30 a.m., I would eat my breakfast and that at 6:00 a.m. sharp we would leave Camp Volckmann and arrive at Camp Utopia that evening.

That evening, while I was resting, a young girl, about 16 years old, carelessly crossed the footbridge.

I said, "Watch your step, Miss. You might stumble."

She stuck her nose in the air. I asked one of the guerrillas who she was. She was identified as Miss Evangeline de Castro, the daughter of the Pay Master of GNL, Volckmann's command.

The order to the Commissary Officer was to prepare my breakfast at 5:00 a.m., an hour before our departure. The *cargadores* must be ready as ordered by the Commanding Officer.

"Yes, sir." the Lieutenant replied. At 4:45 a.m. the next morning I went to the dining hut. There eating were two elderly ladies, and the snobby young girl, and a couple of little kids. One of the older women was the wife of the Pay Master, the mother of Evangeline.

She stood and made sharp remarks to the Commissary Officer, "Did I not tell you that we do not like to eat with enlisted men?"

Now, who is this pointing her finger at me, I thought. I ate my breakfast, not minding the old snob. I didn't care. My concern was focused on the dangerous trails ahead. While I was thinking of more important things, the Lieutenant whispered something to the old woman and suddenly her tone changed from bitter to honey-sweet.

"I am Mrs. de Castro. You know Major de Castro?" she said.

I stood and said, "Yes, Ma'am."

"So, you are from Australia, hey?" she replied. "What an adventure! This is our maid, my two little kids and, of course, Evangeline, my daughter."

Evangeline took my helmet liner and put it on her head. It was smelly from sweat. She slung my M-3 on her shoulder and marched around. "Don't forget me, huh! Don't forget Evangeline! Call me 'Vangie,' and, when the war is finished, come to see us in Manila."

"Where in Manila?" I asked.

The old lady replied, "Everybody knows them. Just ask who are the de Castros."

I learned later that they were wealthy *hacienderos*. Vangie returned my helmet and submachine gun as we were preparing to move out.

"Don't forget us, OK?" she called out.

The snobby mom gave me a hug, and Vangie gave a kiss on the cheek. I counted my cargoes and determined which *cargador* carried which. The final order was that anyone who dropped the radio set would be shot. They nodded their heads and we moved on.

We crossed Trinidad Valley the next day, advancing into the sector of the 66th Infantry Composite commanded by Major Molintas. We spent the night in this area and the next morning continued our trek. US military intelligence sent information to all covert forces in the area to be on the alert for a US soldier in route to the 14th US Infantry and that he should be given all available assistance. On the fourth day of the trek, we were scheduled to cross at 24 kilometers, next to Baguio, but at that point, the Japanese were repairing a bridge damaged by US light bombers. We camped in a ravine about two miles south, where many civilian Filipino's joined us, naively hoping that the single sub-machine gun that I carried would protect all of them from the invaders nearby. I warned my eight men that if we made contact with Japanese forces, they should chase the Filipino civilians away, and, while they were all running, we should all escape from the group, duck into the jungle, and make sure that our cargoes were safe from Japanese view.

At the break of dawn, we felt our way across the rugged jungle terrain until we were near the bridge that was guarded by Japanese troops. The Japanese were alert, yelling out our position and immediately pursuing our group. Our initial plan worked well, for as we ducked into the jungle bushes, the Japanese continued to pursuit the fleeing civilians and they passed right by our positions. We then quickly proceeded to cross the winding trail where we immediately drew fire from another squad. As one gunman could not successfully defend against an entire squad in set battle, we ran. From dawn that morning until 1:30 p.m., the chase continued, with our pursuers firing sporadically.

Suddenly someone yelled, "Halt, who is there!"

Gasping, I pointed at the large US ensignia marked on my holster. Breathing hard, I pointed behind me and yelled, "Japanese!"

We continued running while one platoon of Company L of the 66th Infantry Company intercepted and engaged the Japanese troops. We heard shot fired to the rear of us, and, in what seemed like no time, at all the news came back that all the Japanese were dead.

We continued along the trail. Since they were used to this terrain the native Filipino *cargadores* survived the sharp lava rock with their bare feet, whereas the soles of my brand new paratrooper boots did not. I skidded several times along the way, and, as I recovered my balance, I saw that at that altitude, the cows grazing below looked like the size of flies. One slip would have been enough to end everything. Fortunately, my intensive military training in Australia paid off and I safely traversed through the dangerous high-altitude trail. Two more days on the trail, and it was time for the *cargadores* to return, for we had reached the boundary line between the 66th and 14th US Infantry. My native Filipino *cargadores* were substituted with Christian Filipino soldiers. They could all speak English well, and it was nice to be able to have a long conversation again.

One problem that I did not anticipate was our lack of salt. The Japanese controlled the salt factory in the lowlands, so we were forced to use wild chili peppers to kill the taste of unsalted pork. I ordered the barbecue to burn a little to provide a different taste, as the local help in the temporary message center we had set up was used to eating without salt.

On February 2nd, we caught up with the tail end of the 14th US Infantry, who were in route to a more secure site for the protection of hospital litter cases and to ensure a more centralized command. Among the cases being treated at the time was Major Ferdinand Marcos, a malaria victim.

After putting my radio gear together, I began transmitting all of their messages but I was transmitting at a lower frequency and our signal was weak, so immediately I requisitioned a stronger radio transceiver. The next day a small military cub plane dropped a little parachute with our radio. I was very happy that they had sent the most modern and powerful radio.

Two days later I received orders to proceed to Nanzabitan area to join the 3rd Battalion, 14th Infantry, USAFE. Unfortunately, this meant another week of enduring leeches and enduring the wet and cold jungle and mountains. Our orders were to remain undetected and to avoid Japanese patrols. The mission was always more important than the elimination of a few enemy soldiers.

In the afternoon of the day we were to leave, Colonel Manriquez the Commanding Officer, Major Dingkong the Executive Officer, and Major Marcos came, shook my hands and wished me good fortune. Along with a armed military escort, I had two *cargadores*, Allaga and Bomalliag, and I was very lucky to have them. They were hunters and knew every inch of the terrain.

That night we crossed a sweet potato plantation where everything looked normal but, earlier that evening from this location, the Japanese arose and assaulted our party and killed one guerrilla from our unit.

The pressure was on as Japanese patrols were coming our way, and the CO of E Company let us know that he could no longer provide an armed escort. We snuck out at midnight, and floated down the stream on a fairly large log. The Japanese were noisy along the river, and we easily passed them. When we hit the trail, I was cold so we ran to keep warm.

The following afternoon, we reached a village the Japanese had not penetrated. We had followed a stream for about two hours, leaving no tracks so we knew that we were fairly secure. The chief of the village was friendly and, fortunately, my *cargadores* spoke the local dialect. All I had to offer the chief was moldy cigarettes, but we were received warmly and fed.

The following day we were given a half-dozen hard-boiled eggs and one live chicken. We were escorted to the stream nearby, which we followed, until we arrived at a foot trail. We stopped for the night in a place that contained many stranded Filipino natives. I asked my two guides why these natives were stranded and was told that the boulders and heavy brush blocked out the sun, and caused the trail to be too dark to continue. It was necessary to build torches to light our way so we could continue the next day. I insisted upon staying toward the front for through experience, I had learned that at the rear of the group, the trail would be well trampled and muddy.

By noon we had chopped through the enormous mass of brush and, vines and finally saw the sunlight. We stopped to clean out leeches. One was already full of blood behind my ear lobe, while another was inside my right boot. How it got there, I do not know.

On the sixth day we heard dogs barking and encountered a small village. We followed a trail leading away from the village and within an hour and a half a voice shouted, "Halt!"

I sent one of my guides with a note: "A member of the Allied Intelligence Bureau (AIB) is on the way to your camp."

The guide came back with an officer, a 1st Lieutenant to escort me to the camp. The camp was clean and in ship-shape, because the Filipino soldiers thought the member of AIB was a GI from Australia. They were disappointed when they saw a flat nosed, short, brown soldier. But when they heard my accent, they hesitated and called me "Sir."

Captain Mabonga was out on a field mission. He and Company I went to meet a group of Japanese stragglers. The Executive Officer, Captain

Gregorio Montejo, had to open and read my sealed orders in the absence of Captain Mabonga. My orders were to determine the true activities of the Japanese forces in the Balete Pass near the Baguio area.

Intelligence reports had shown the presence of a very large Japanese battalion moving south every night for the past month. If the count was correct, there were enough enemy soldiers concentrated in the area to push the whole of the allied forces back to the sea. Two well-experienced reconnaissance boys took me to a place that had a commanding view of the area, which was on top of a very large boulder. We observed and reported three Japanese rifle companies moving south during the night verified the reports we had received.

The following day I looked at pictures of Japanese uniforms in order to better identify the troops I had observed earlier and a green patch with an oak leaf attracted my attention. We went back to verify the tell-tale insignia. We determined that the Japanese troops were the same fresh division that that had landed in the Philippines a few months back. We changed position the next evening, crossed the highway toward the eastern side of the valley, and continued our reconnaissance. Japanese troops of similar uniform and number were also moving in this area, but with a major distinction, they were moving *northward!* This was a topic of discussion in the deduction room of US headquarters.

Induction and Deduction

It was confirmed by General MacArthur's headquarters (G.H.Q. Base I) at Holandia that the same outfit moved south one night, rested the next night, and then returned to the north on the third evening. The conclusion was that the Japanese were putting on a show to camouflage a weak position. Consequently American forces were ordered to cross Balete Pass and did so with very little resistance.

We could see that the Japanese were disorganized. They appeared in small groups on almost every trail, disturbing the natives and causing them to seek refuge within our military areas. In March and April, we all felt very worried by the increased Japanese presence. A movement of Japanese troops, approximately of platoon size, was sighted following the trail to our headquarters and emergency evacuation was ordered. We moved to the alternate campsite, which was always on hand for such cases, evacuating hospital staff and patients first, followed by battalion headquarters personnel.

This was my night. I was a US G.I. and the soldiers looked to my experience for leadership and support. I move forward to the front line. At least it was a relief to know that the boys were veterans of the jungle. We plotted the ambush along Balete Pass, went to the selected area and deployed each man, knowing that the Japanese did not travel in the dark. Both the submachine gunner and the Sergeant remained close to me. There was a gate at the opposite end of the clearing we had chosen, about 75 yards from where I was located. The submachine gun, M-1 rifle, and the Enfields were pointed toward the gate, while the carbines on the upper embankment were spaced about five paces apart between men and trained on the path below. We knew that when the Japanese arrived, we would be breathing right down their necks.

I gave the order, "Nobody fires before I do."

It was daybreak when the Japanese soldiers appeared, and we could barely see their faces, while they were under the shadow of the trees. Everyone was holding his breath. I drew my .45 and waited until the lead man was in my direct line of sigh. I fired once and everyone opened up with their weapons. There were a few who escaped the string of sub-machine gun bursts. They were at first lucky, but then the M-1s and Enfields fired and picked them up.

I yelled, "Freeze! Don't move!"

We waited until we were sure there were no Japanese moving. They were known to be very tricky, sometimes pretending to be dead, while waiting to pick a target, shoot and kill at least once more before dying. The battle area became known as "death valley."

The evacuation party all moved out of the area, but we had to remain in this place called Binalian. We had to wait until all the new huts are ready before we move to Nambolosan. At dusk, a runner arrived.

"More Japanese on the way, Sir," was his report.

"About how many?" I asked.

"About a hundred," he answered.

When a civilian says a hundred, it could mean less than half. Again we prepared for the arrival of the Japanese soldiers. Filipino grave diggers ran from Death Valley when they heard of on-coming Japanese soldiers. The burial mission was not completed.

The site where the Japanese troops currently were was close to our camp. We didn't lose anytime, and immediately took off to meet them. This time it was not an ambush.

The Japanese soldiers knew we were coming. They can see us approaching. It was sunset, and our scout also warned us where the Japanese were. The trails are narrow and the pampas are thick. We were going down on an angle, and there the Japanese soldiers were. For a while there was shooting, but when the situation quickly became a hand-to-hand engagement.

Bolos, samurais and bayonets went into action. Even the Japanese knew better than shooting in the dark. One might kill his own comrade. The Japanese soldiers were very aggressive. They didn't give an inch.

A soldier with a samurai sword swung at me. He aimed at my mid-section. I swung my bolo toward the same direction hoping to cut his arm. He missed. I also missed. My delivery was a horizontal blow. He came back with another horizontal back hand. I felt a rip on the front portion of my fatigue shirt. I pulled my stomach back as I delivered a flashing downward follow blow. I missed him again.

Old man Benigno Ramos to my left just downed his last Japanese soldier. Now he came to my rescue. He pushed me down. I laid flat on a shrub. Old man Benigno ducked under the heavy Japanese number one blow, at a fraction of a second the old man launched a heavy follow blow striking the back of the Japanese head. The Japanese soldier's head was almost severed. I sat up wet from sweating.

The night was cold most especially in higher elevation, and once in a while there is a little frost on top of some old log lying in the open. The yelling was changing into laughter, as the boys search the Japanese for goodies and souvenirs. Benigno and another boy pulled me up.

"It's finished, Sir," was their report.

I was ashamed. I didn't say a word. We went back to camp. It was dark and we had to feel our way back. I caught a few stickers in my right ear and on the back of my right hand, some varieties of rattan are full of stickers.

The following morning a runner came to report that our huts were ready. I checked on my shirt and saw a rip about six inches long. That was the thud I felt last night. I didn't feel right.

Every one of the boys had two or three kills. They teased the boys with only one kill. They were talking about how many throats they chopped, how may arms and legs were cut off, even how many heads were cut off. I didn't have any, not one. I felt I was left out.

One of the radio code clerks was cleaning my .45 and cleaning out the dirt and leaves in the pockets of my fatigue shirt. We never tuck our shirts into the trousers. It's better for the shirt pockets to scoop dirt than the belt and waistband of the pants. There are leeches, centipedes, and one has no time to pull his pants down to remove the blood-suckers, not on the battle ground. The old man turned to me with a snide look. I knew it was for me, and I was a little sensitive about what happened only a few hours before.

Finally he said with a consoling tone, "Sir, don't feel bad it's always that way at first, at least you are still with us."

When we got to the secondary headquarters the S-2, Lt. Lino Patajo along with the battalion XO sent two experienced boys back to Binalian to put a couple of grenades under the eaves of the huts. The grenades were bound with a small dried vine to secure the lever. He then pulled out the safety pins. He was setting a booby trap. When the Japanese burned down the huts, which is their habit, the vines would burn out and the grenade will explode.

The old man Benigno Ramos was assigned to me as my orderly. It was confided that this old man was a professional escrima teacher before the outbreak of the war. He carried a very long bolo, not on his hip but under his left armpit, the belt slung over the right shoulder. The bolo cannot be drawn out like other bolo's because it is extra long. This scabbard opens on the side so the long blade can be unsheathed in a flash.

While doing other chores in the message center, Benigno the orderly gradually eased along the idea of me rehearsing some more in the use of the bolo. He said that it is important to him that I must live longer because my job in the message center is vital.

"With all the hardships you went through," he said. "You deserve to live a little longer." He insisted that I needed a little more exercise in the use of the bolo. "The use of the baton (stick) is a little different. If you get hit with a baton, you can always get up. With the bolo there is no second chance."

I nodded my head looking at him more seriously. "How much experience do you have in the Art?" I interjected.

He answered, "I had fifteen years teaching experience before the outbreak of the war. I know you have a little or maybe enough knowledge in the art, but as I watched you that night, some things are missing. You lacked the aggressiveness, and this is common when you are half-afraid.

"One thing you must fix in your mind, Sir, you are afraid," he continued. "The Japanese is also afraid but he doesn't know that you know that. Knowing this fact, you must take advantage of his weak points. One who fears injury much more so than death is always on the defensive. You can not win a bout in combat by defensive moves all the time."

"So what should be done?" I asked.

"You know enough of the art," he assured me. "You don't need to know too much. Knowing the basic flows is sufficient. Timing and determination. Determination to take another life. That's better than giving up yours. In order to build your courage, you need to experience the sight of a sharp blade passing by your body and face once in a while, in front of your stomach occasionally so that you can gage your distance and become effective."

"While giving me that training," I asked. "What happens if you miscalculate and rip my stomach open?"

"Unless I intend to lay the blade on you," he replied. "You'll never be hit."

"And what will happen if by accident I cut you, any part of your body I asked?"

"I'll give you one month's pay," he assured me.

The exercises began, but I didn't have the taste for it. The rest of the boys induced me, "Go ahead, Sir. You'll appreciate it one day."

The exercise was disrupted by a messenger. "More Japanese coming, Sir."

"Where and how big is the group?"

He replied with the usual, "One hundred."

This time the Japanese troops were on the trail toward the old camp. "No attack" was the order that came from Capt. Montejo. The information was flashed by radio to the next company guarding the old trail about 2 days away. Around sunset time, the natives were pointing toward the old camp. There were lots of flames lighting up the night. In a few seconds a big blast echoed across the range. The booby trap had gone off. The following day a coded message came across the radio: Only 2 Japanese were found dead. "It's not worth it," I said. "Two hand grenades are more costly than only two Japanese."

When we transmitted all the messages to GHQ, we relaxed a little. One message came back. GHQ wanted to know where is the assembly point of the retreating Japanese troops. GHQ's message was relayed to all sub-stations. In the meantime, the escrima exercises with old man Benigno continued. I kept wondering if this bolo rehearsal would help at all.

Another group of Japanese stragglers was reported. Only a dozen, the report stated, that's all. That small group could be an advance party for a larger body, but as it turned out, it wasn't, which sure was a relief. A squad went to take care of them.

Everyday this month of March 1945, there were Japanese soldiers on practically every trail. The Americans were on the main road in the central valley, which is why the Japanese took to the hills. There was peace in the low lands, but we had more trouble now than anytime of the year. The Japanese soldiers were weak, tired and very hungry.

The feeling of going to encounter the enemy is like going out to the field to pick tomatoes. When it's finished, we will go back, wash our hands, wash all the blood stains before we eat and then think of how we escaped with our lives.

I was getting bored, but I always had the cobwebs in my stomach while in action. Toward the middle of the month of March was Easter. A little cub plane flew overhead and dropped a little parachute and inside was a pair of slightly used shoes for me. The sole of my only pair was at its last layer. Sometimes, I feel the gravel poke my right foot. With the pair of shoes was a brown envelope with all of my mail. One important mail was from my mother. She was still alive, so were my father, sisters and brothers, except a sister who died from a witchcraft spell. There were bottles of Atabrine, quinine, iodine crystals and a .45, which I had requisitioned because I loaned my .45 to a captain, but he got killed in action. I had written to my mother a year ago while in Santa Cruz, Ilocos Sur, and I was only now getting a reply.

This time the Japanese forces were giving us too much pressure. We had to abandon Nambolosan. We moved to a higher elevation, a flat side of the mountain called Oliweg. There a few months ago, Filipino guerrillas built a little airstrip where a small cub plane can land. The Japanese must have known about it, and they keep trying to climb the trail and reach the airstrip. But Japanese troops could not climb the trail because of the extreme difficulty of the terrain. To reach the airstrip ourselves, we had to scramble up on vines and climb vertically for about 30 feet. Since they could not reach the airstrip, the Japanese decided to bombard us with mortar fire. We avoided the mortar shells by staying in caves, and we were able to have our radio transceiver installed, but we were on the wrong side of the mountain for a good radio transmission.

We had to move out. Two boys with a dozen Filipino natives went to Banaue. There use to be a few huts when company K occupied the place. All it needed was a few repairs and cleaning out. Our battalion consisted of 2 platoons of riflemen plus about a platoon of administrative personnel. I had 6 radio operators and code clerks plus 2 orderlies. While in Banaue, we barely had the time to exercise. We were always on alert. This time we were capturing Filipinos who were working for the Japanese military as guides and collaborators. There was even a couple of UN (*United Nippon*) similar to our FBI. I have more compassion for the Japanese soldiers because they are bound by Army rules like us. Japanese soldiers have to fight and be killed if necessary. But I had no compassion for these Filipino traitors who helped the Japanese destroy our land, killed our brothers, sisters and parents. These lowly traitors do not deserve to live, do not deserve even the trouble of holding a court martial to convict them. My sharp bolo was always ready for their throats.

Because of the elevation and contours of this knoll, a system had to be devised to guard all the trails. There are only 2 platoons of fighting men to stop the Japanese, plus a handful of non-combatants, although they too must fight. We learned that General Yamashita selected Kiangan, Ifugao Province to be the final stand of the Japanese army. The rest of the Japanese forces were desperate, and they took any trail leading to Kiangan according to their maps. The other Japanese unit commanders depended on the success of Yamashita to hold his ground so they can determine when to send reinforcements, so Yamashita's actions may be just a delaying action.

The Japanese soldiers came in early June. It was a rainy day when a large unit of Japanese soldiers charged against our position. When the Japanese soldiers charged, they yelled, "Banzai!" which meant, "Long Live the Emperor!" But it also meant that they were fighting to the death. When the Japanese attack came, we had organized our unit to guard the trails. We were on a wedge formation: One man must be on the front as point, and the two others were on each side, standing a little to the rear. I took the point on the uppermost trail. I choose the highest trail because by the time the Japanese soldiers got to the top, they were already tired. Second, any attacking enemy that slipped had to roll down instead of up, and he will become the problem of the men on the next trail below. Like any Banzai charge, the Japanese are always noisy. They were yelling and shouting as they charged. The Japanese were not afraid to die. If they don't charge, their officers will chop off their heads. So the Japanese soldiers had to charge whether they liked it or not.

The Filipino guerrillas, on the other hand, chewed their tobacco, grit their teeth and swung their bolos, chopping here and jabbing there. Filipino soldiers used long bolos, short daggers, pointed bamboo, and pulverized chili peppers with sand deposited in bamboo tubes to spray towards the enemy so they could not see. By now my adrenaline was really up.

One bayonet and samurai sword came at me simultaneously. The samurai sword was in front of me while the bayonet was a little to the left. With my left hand I parried the bayonet. Then I blocked the sword coming down on me. As the bayonet man went by, his body came in line with my bolo, and I slashed down to cut his left hip. The samurai attacker was coming back with a backhand blow, but I met his triceps with the bolo blade. His arm fell to the ground. He yelled at himself for his mistake, "*Bakatare!*" "Stupid!" As I advanced forward, the men on each side finished him off. Another samurai attacker came at me. I did an inside block and snapped a hit on his stomach. But my bolo bounced off. The soldier was wearing a heavy leather pack strapped to his shoulder. I returned with a strike to the back of his knee, and he fell. I advanced forward. More Japanese soldiers were coming up the trail, many of them skidding in the muddy terrain. Each time an attacker skid, he went tumbling down the trail. In the battle, as boots stomped on the mud, the trails became muddier and more slippery than ever. The upper trails were cleared of the enemy, while down below were more clashing and clanking of steel. More fighting. More yelling. Mostly, Japanese soldiers yelling.

When the battle ended, I wiped my face with my left hand to clear my eyes from the rain and mud, and I found bloodstains on my face. The boys told me, "Blood, Sir." These Filipino soldiers could just see as well in the dark, as if it were daylight. Their eyes had adapted to the darkness beneath the thick jungle canopy. They could see the difference between rainwater and blood. I felt a twitch on the flesh underneath my left palm when I parried the bayonet attack. I didn't know I was cut. It was getting sore. In a few minutes I smelled burning hair. I wondered what it was. One of the older men put the ashes along with the remaining unburned hair on my cut. The blood stopped running from my palm. Later I learned that it was the old man's pubic hair that he had clipped and burned. He learned this medical remedy while studying escrima at an early childhood age. "Cured my cut with his pubic hair and a prayer?" I said and laughed. But it stopped the flow of blood. Along the trail, we were encountering Japanese stragglers every day.

Eventually, I had to take sick leave, so I stayed with the clerks at the message center. "Why did I go to the frontlines," the clerks asked. "Where the fighting took place when I did not have to?" I didn't say much, but I felt more comfortable with the fighting men. Noncombatants clerks can get in trouble just as much.

After a week of sick leave, a report came that Japanese soldiers took over the opposite side of the mountain range. We were on the west, and a good two thousand yards to the east Japanese forces took over three villages. On the extreme right is Nambolosan where we were last March. On the extreme left is Nagtopakan and between the two is Macdo. We used to send a detail of men to fire a few shots at the Japanese camps at night so the soldiers could not rest. The Japanese unit was a big group and must have been at least regimental size. The Japanese didn't even bother to move after the Filipino detail fired a few shots. Instead, before the Japanese unit went to sleep, at dusk every automatic weapon fired at the near by bushes for about three minutes, then they settle down and went to sleep.

Captain Gregorio Montejo was now the battalion commander and he had a conference with his staff officers, but no one could suggest a good plan to drive the Japanese unit away. The Filipino natives of the three villages were now under the care of Montejo's battalion. One morning after all the radio messages were dispatched, an old hunter came up with an idea. Our side of the mountain had a clearing of about a hundred yards long. The idea was to make as many torches as we can and parade them. One torch to a man at about ten paces apart. These torches are clearly visible to the Japanese at night. All the native men even with a few young girls participated. The girls lit the torches one after another, and some chopped more pinewood to make more torches. When the head torch man reaches the end of the clearing he enters a trail to pick up another torch and go back to the starting point. The same twenty or thirty people paraded all night. To the Japanese there probably appeared to be thousands of torches that went to the same direction and it's logical to believe that these torches were guerillas on their way to where the rest of their outfits were. At daybreak Filipino scouts were sent to survey the situation. The scouts came back shaking their heads. "No more Japanese, Sir," was their report. Now, the Filipino civilians from the three villages can go home, so they can resume bringing in food supplies to us.

After two days another large group of Japanese soldiers were on our trail, coming through Banaue this time. While knocking down antennas, packing radios, typewriters and records, a small guerrilla patrol arrived in camp and reported to the Captain. They were from Company K and were cut off by the Japanese. They had to circle around to our sector. A few of them are Christians. They helped us carry our packs. We moved to Babaddi, a little higher than Banaue, a little to the southwest about four hours hike on the winding trails. It was apparent that the Japanese could see our food supply drop area because we learned of another site using the same identification codes. On Mondays we displayed our panels to form the letter L. On Tuesday maybe E. On Wednesday X and so on. We were being copied by the Japanese. The boys had to clear an area on the opposite side away from the observation of the Japanese binoculars.

Three days later, about the end of June, a small Japanese group was sighted an hour away from our camp. We went to check on them but the soldiers were in a deep ravine, and we couldn't smoke them out. The boys were getting concerned for as long as there are enemy troops close by, no one can rest. On the opposite side of the draw two boys with carbines were descending. I yelled, "Stop! Don't take a chance!" But the boys were too brave, or maybe they didn't hear me. Jaime Abasolo was shot with a pistol on the side of his left chest and the bullet was taken out of the right side of the abdomen. I was told the Japanese soldiers were crawling away from the ravine. The Japanese that shot him must have been an officer because it was a Lugar bullet that was taken out of him. The boys were discouraged. No one wanted to go down to the ravine. There was only one thing to do. It was getting late, nearing sunset. I called three good shots with Enfield rifles and told them to pick out good spots and remain. We carried Jaime and withdrew. In twenty minutes six shots were heard from the Enfield rifles, and later two-dozen native Filipinos carried the six dead Japanese on litters. They had to be brought to HQ for investigation. There were maps found on the Japanese, and the trails dotted with lines leading to Kiangan. That was a sad day for us because Jaime was always singing when we were resting. He was only 17 years old. He was a fast code clerk and a good soldier and a friend. We buried him near our camp with a full military service.

A new order by radiogram came ordering us to move out of the hills and join HQ 14th Infantry which was now located in the low land in the town of Bagabag, Nueva Viscaya. The same day while we were packing, three unarmed Taiwanese arrived and surrendered. They claimed they had to kill their Japanese captain. "No eat, too much work," the Taiwanse men said. "Me labor battalion, no soldier, no gun." We let them carry some of our heavy loads.

At The Low Lands

As we were approaching the town of Pingkian, we carried a white flag. The American GIs were running like jackrabbits into their foxholes below. There were about three hundred of us including civilians and the families of the guerrillas. I looked ahead with my binoculars and saw the 20th US Infantry Regiment. As we got closer, I yelled, "I saw you in Hunter Liggett two years ago." Hunter Liggett is near King City, California. Some of the GIs waived their hands and shouted, "FILIPINO GIs!" Some of the sergeants were still distrustful. We bivouacked by the riverbank. The boys formed three columns broken in platoons. I called, "Attention!" The Filipino boys were sharp, very sharp. Poorly dressed, no shoes, but the American G.I.'s were amazed. "Godamned!" the G.I.s said. "No shoes but their heels clicked." These are real soldiers left over from different outfits that did not surrender to the Japanese. We were all very proud to be soldiers of the United States of America. We were all fighting for the same cause. The American G.I.'s were ordered to stay away, but later the boys were eating chocolate bars. I and the battalion CO entered the orderly tent of the 20th infantry saluted the American Captain inside, and then I introduced Captain Montejo.

"I'm Sergeant Leovigildo Giron, A.I.B."

The Captain asks, "What is that?"

"Allied Intelligence Bureau," I said.

"Never heard of it," he responded.

A Major entered the tent so I saluted.

He looked at me twice and asked, "Are you one of the boys at Volckmann's camp?" I recognized the Major. He was Captain Vaughan when we first met and now was a Major.

"What can I do for you son?" He inquired.

"I want food for about three hundred soldiers and civilians."

The American Captain interrupted and said in a sharp tone, "Why don't you go back to the jungle where you belong!"

"Do you have a name, Captain?" I inquired, but Major Vaughan pulled the snobby Captain to the corner of the tent and whispered something to him. The Captain turned to me and said, "So you are MacArthur's boy, huh? Okay, we will see what we can do for your boys."

He prepared a requisition form as I was introducing Captain Montejo to Major Vaughn. Vaughn asked, "What happened to you, Sergeant Giron? All of a sudden you were gone. Where did you go? We were together during the bombardment of Lingayen and Baguio almost a year ago."

I signed the form and the Captain said, "Give us an hour."

Major Vaughn and I jumped into his jeep when I told him I have three prisoners. Captain Montejo stayed to handle the distribution of food supplies. The Major and I drove to Solano with the three Taiwanese workers to the 6th Division G.H.Q., G-3 H.Q.

"What do you have here Vaughan?" an old gray-haired man inquired. He was a one star General. Major Vaughan and I saluted. The General asked me bluntly, "When were you with Whitney last?"

"August 1944," I answered.

"Do you know he is now a two star general?"

"No, Sir."

The supply sergeant pushed a receipt over the table and said, "There you are son, three prisoners, and this is your receipt. Your food supplies are now on the way."

Major Vaughan tapped me on the shoulder and said, "I told you we will take good care of you."

The general said, "Yes, Sir, anytime. You boys did a good job."

We went back to our bivouac area. I and the battalion S-2 1st Lieutenant Lino Patajo slept side by side, Captain Montejo was called on the loud speaker. The loud speaker continued, "Transportation for civilians first. First truck to Solano, next truck, still Solano. Third was for Bayombong, the fourth and fifth and the two last for Bambang." In an hour the same trucks hauled us to Bagabag. We got to the Regimental H.Q. and the order was changed. The little town of Bagabag was too small for all the American G.I.'s and Filipino guerrillas. A couple of bombs can kill too many so we were ordered back to Bambang. We occupied the public market. July went by and we all moved to Kiangan. That brought us closer to the final line of defense of the Japanese. We got there in time to bury dead Japanese. The American G.I.'s sprayed the whole town with DDT. There were many large green flies and maggots crawling in the mouths and eyes of the dead Japanese soldiers.

After a week it rained. The civilians warned us that Japanese soldiers love to come down and spray the town with machine gun bullets. "They are crazy," the Filipino civilians said. Heeding their warning, at night we wore our rain gear and hid behind logs and large rocks. All of the sudden a carbine fired all fourteen rounds in the magazine. Then the machine guns opened fire. Japanese machine guns. The next morning one of Sergeant's carbines was almost cut in two when a samurai sword swung at him. Sergeant blocked the blade with his carbine and the muzzle was almost cut off. He then pumped all fourteen rounds into the Japanese soldier.

The Japanese must have sensed that there was more resistance in Kiangan besides the American G.I.'s. The American occupied the open area below Kiangan about five hundred yards. Their howitzers kept firing all night so no one could sleep. Two days later we went on patrol. I don't know why I consented to go when there are now more guerrillas. The Regimental H.Q. and the 3rd battalion are here, but the 1st and 2nd Battalions were still in the hills. Because operation of a C-100 walkie-talkie was not familiar to the boys in the message center, I was convinced to try it out. I was the only one that knows how to operate the walkie-talkie. I found out that in Panopdopan where in 2nd Battalion was dispersed, there was an airfield. A C-47 cargo plane had been landing bringing food supplies and G.I. uniforms. The Japanese really wanted this place. The 2nd Battalion had their good share of troubles. They needed an air strike, which is why the C-100 radio was needed to guide the airplanes. The order was to burn all the uniforms and food supplies. To one side of the airstrip was a rice field flooded with water about three feet deep and in some places deeper. We noticed G.I.'s in brand new greens wading toward the strip. The guerrillas jumped and met the soldiers in greens. "Why the scramble?" I asked. One sergeant, a native, fixed his rifle and bayonet, slung it on his shoulder and stood still. Now, he said, "Compare the length of mine and their bayonets." That's when I noticed that the American bayonet equals the height of the helmet or just barely above it. The men in brand-new green uniforms in the rice field had their rifle and bayonet also slung on their shoulders but the bayonets were way above their helmets. "What does that prove?" I asked. The sergeant picked a captured Japanese rifle and bayonet and carried it on his shoulder. The bayonet was very long. It was a dead give away. The guerrillas went to action with bolos. It's hard to shoot them because the Japanese were crouched in the water with only their helmets standing above the protruding rice blades. Machine guns cannot shoot down ward, the guerrillas might be hit.

Two of the boys, one on each side, removed their shirts, secured it to the rifle like a scarecrow to attract the attention of the Japanese. They will emerge from the water to shoot. The rest of the guerrillas picked them off with their rifles, one by one. There were three or four that surrendered, but I think they were too much trouble to be brought out of the rice fields.

American planes were strafing the Japanese position below on the opposite side. We left the knoll while it was ablaze. The smell of burning rice and flesh was in the air.

We set camp near the edge of the clearing under a big fir tree, and we had a clear view of whatever moved in the open. I dug me a foxhole but it was a little tight and uncomfortable.

There were tree roots too tough to chop with my shovel and too congested to swing a bolo knife. I removed my canteen and placed it on the edge. I held my .45 while I crouched to take a rest. Once in a while, I heard shots. These were Japanese rifle shots. They always had a double sound, "peek-boom." That "peek-boom" sound was always a Japanese rifle. There were too many shots being fired, and I couldn't sleep or even take a rest. I felt water dripping. It was not raining. That's when I discovered my canteen was punctured. The following morning we learned one native got shot trying to move his bowels away from his foxhole. We believed another guerrilla shot him. The password that night was *carabao*. When challenged with the word "carabao," one should answer, *sangol* (yoke). We left the area as the boys took turns to carry the dead soldier back to Kiangan. I let another carry the C-100 radio. I brought back the punctured canteen to show the boys. An American G.I. offered 300 pesos for the useless canteen. I asked him what he was going to do with it. He said he is retiring and he wants to show it to his girl friend how close a Japanese bullet came to him.

Thirty-Four Years Old

On August 18th I requested a three-day leave to go to Bayombong to visit my friends. They were members of our Secret Service. They begged me to go see them on my birthday, August 20, 1945. I will be 34 years old in two days (fig. 2). I regretted taking that leave. Between Kiangan and Bagabag was about half a day's hike. The US Army engineers were constructing new roads, and Japanese snipers were also busy taking pot shots at the caterpillar drivers.

My Khakis were clean, but when the Japanese snipers started shooting, I had to dump myself in a depression for cover. A jeep came with G.I.'s armed with M-1s and light machine guns. They went after the sniper. My pants and shirt were soiled. In Bayombong my friends had to wash them for me that afternoon.

Before dark they were dry. The news got around so the following day we were at the house of one of the Secret Service agents. We had lunch. There were maybe 20 high school girls cooking and serving. I ate everything. It was food I missed so much since I left for America 19 years ago. An old lady said, "Eat all you can. You haven't eaten these foods since you left this country." After lunch we went to the market to buy fruits. Mangoes, *lansones* and other Filipino fruits that were not raised in America. I made 300 pesos from the sale of my punctured water canteen so I could afford the food. I was staying with Rosita Bonaneg was one of the (SS) agents and her family. She was a young schoolteacher who eventually choose to become a nun.

Fig. 2—Sergeant Leo M. Giron.

AIB vs. CIC

On the way back from the market, a Filipino lawyer named Manalo attached to the CIC (Counter Intelligence Company) stopped me and wanted to confiscate my .45 side arm. I slapped his hand and said, "Hold it, Son." I patted my cowhide holster and said, "I can use this piece real well." He claimed I should not be carrying a pistol that only officers were allowed to carry side arms. I answered, "Like hell I can't!" A US Army Corporal, a tall skinny blond in charge of the CIC detachment, came down from the bamboo house overlooking us on the street and asked Manalo, "What's wrong?"

Manalo responded, "He's carrying a side arm."

The Corporal asked, "Are you an American G.I.?"

"Certainly!" I replied.

"How come you are dressed like that?"

"I've been with the guerrilla outfit for almost two years now this is all I've got."

"What happened to your holster?" he asked.

"Lost in night operations."

"How can you lose a holster piece?"

"We were swimming across a river on a raft," I replied. "The raft got shot we dove under. We lost everything." I might have had more trouble telling him I loaned it and the Lieutenant got killed.

"What's your outfit?"

I said, "A.I.B. Allied Intelligence Bureau."

The Corporal wanted to see my dog tags. Manalo insisted the Philippine Army had dog tags also like mine.

The Corporal looked at my dog tags and exclaimed, "How about that!?" The tall blond Corporal asked once more, "How did you come to this country?"

I replied, "By submarine. Almost 2 years ago." The corporal grabbed Monalo by the neck of his shirt and took him away. The two girls carrying my basket full of fruits revealed that Manalo is courting one of them, which is why he had stopped and interrogated me. The following day, I waved good-bye to my friends and hitched a ride with a US Army 6th Division truck. The truck was going my way. After telling him my outfit, the driver took me all the way to Kiangan. I was grateful. He said he met some of the Filipino boys in Camp Murphy. "They are nice boys," he assured me. "Good fighters."

On September 9th about a week before the surrender of General Yamashita, I was recalled to G-3 General Head Quarters in Manila. I went to the Recreational Department (REC-DEPT) 6th Division for a ride. There a sergeant said, "I'm making the run to Manila tomorrow. Be here at 6 a.m." At 5:30 a.m. I was there. The sentry escorted me to the sergeant. "He is OK," said the Sarg. "He is riding with me."

By late-breakfast we were in Manila. I had some more money left of my 300 pesos. I didn't spend too much in Bayombong. I still have about 220 pesos. I treated the Sergeant to breakfast. We ordered ham and eggs, toast and coffee. The sergeant gave me a funny look.

After we finished our breakfast, I asked the waitress, "How much?"

"Only two hundred pesos, Sir."

Wow! I was in luck that I had enough money.

"Where did you get that much money in the jungle?" the Sergeant asked.

"I sold my punctured canteen for 300 pesos."

"You could have asked for a thousand," the sergeant said. "Now the man can brag about how close he came to a Japanese. Maybe he didn't even smell one."

Jungle Freedom to Classical Military Life

About 2:30 p.m. I was in G-3 where Major Williams took me to the clearing section. A Sergeant greeted me, "Welcome back." I politely nodded with a smile. Major Williams picked up the telephone and then he took me outside to wait for the commissary personnel to pick me up. As I was sitting on my pack a couple of MPs came to ask me where I came from. Before I could jump up a Two Star General walked in and announced, "At ease." Then he turned to me and asked, "Are there anymore fighting up north?"

"Yes, Sir, especially at night. They always love to spray the town with machine gun fire."

"They do, huh? Those slant-eyed leeches will soon surrender. Your comrades are in Camp Murphy. After you eat, somebody will take you there." Then the General looked at me and said, "I didn't salute anybody for a long time. No one salutes in the front."

When the General left, three more MPs came asking if I ever got to fight with the Japanese.

"Yes, for about a year, a little less," I answered.

"How many did you kill?" one MP inquired.

"I don't know. When you fire a machine gun you cannot count how many bullets are yours and how many from your comrades. The Japanese soldiers are full of holes, and its impossible to tell who made the holes."

"Did you use the carbine?" another asked.

The other MP said with reprimanding tone, "He said he used a machine gun, dummy. That's a carbine, not a machine gun."

"Which is your favorite weapon? An M-1, a sub or carbine?"

"I don't like carbines. It doesn't shoot far. I didn't have an M-1. I used an M-3 submachine gun and my bolo knife."

"Bolo? That's the long butcher knife," the other MP said.

The sergeant hushed them. "Don't you know these Filipino boys can make that bolo knife talk?"

A chubby fellow broke in. The MP boys said, "Hi, Fatso. Did you eat all them round steaks?"

"Nope. But this boy will, he replied, pointing at me. "Your name *Leo-bagaldo Guy-ron?*"

"That's me."

"Follow me." I jumped into the weapons carrier, threw in my pack and carbine and away we all drove off. Two blocks away and somebody opened the screen door. A man in white apron and a regular cook's hat pointed at the steaks, round steaks as big as diapers, and said, "Pick your choice."

"That one!" I pointed.

"Flour or not?"

"Never mind," said the driver, "Just cook it. This boy looks hungry. Make it well done. Filipinos don't like raw meat. They saw a lot of Japanese raw meat."

When the cooked steaks arrived, I ate and ate. There was grease all over my lips and chin. "One more?" the cook asked.

"No," I shook my head.

"More milk then. It's good for you." He poured another glassful. By then I can feel my navel stretching. I've never eaten that good before. I could hardly breathe. I belched and the sergeant said, "There you go. You feel better now? How about some pie?"

"How can I refuse a piece of pie."

"What kind?"

"Any kind," I said.

"You're not too hard to please," the cook replied.

The sergeant tapped me on the shoulder pointing to his left. "That's the latrine. After that big steak and that pie you want to go there. When you get through, I'll take you to Camp Murphy." It was already dark when we went there. Both of us went to the orderly tent. The C.O. took me to my assigned tent. I shook hands with the sergeant and said, "Thanks." "I'm obliged," he answered. After I fixed my bunk and then washed up a little, I went to the Day Room. I was greeted by a voice that said, "I thought you were dead Giron? We heard while you were in route to ZRF. Balete pass, that you were captured."

"How did you hear that?" I asked.

Rufino "Pee Wee" Duran said laughing, "You dumb bastards, you believe all kinds of shit regardless." We laughed and we greeted each other. I was back in civilization again. Dominos, black jack, poker game, seven eleven, you name it. There's life again, a different kind of living. Somebody yelled, "Attention!" A 2nd Lieutenant poked his nose in the door. "Let the Lieutenant in and see his luck in the black jack table."

"No thanks," Lieutenant said. "I want to see Sergeant Giron."

It was 2nd Lieutenant Guyot, but he was a sergeant when I knew him. He was also my brother in the lodge.

"I'll come to pick you up tomorrow," Guyot said. "Our outfit is in San Miguel, Tarlac. The 978th Signal Service Company Provisional is now a separate outfit. The Recon will be disbanded soon." Recon meant the 1st Filipino Reconnaissance Battalion."

"No more Bahala Na unit?" I asked.

"Still is but they are now a separate command."

The next morning after breakfast, the Lieutenant came and he asked, "How do you like it? Son-of-a-bitch, don't they ever forget that lousy reveille?" He almost died laughing. We left for our outfit, and in about 45 minutes we arrived. Sergeant Tanato, now promoted to the rank of Master Sergeant, was waiting for us. Tanto pointed to the orderly room. I went in, stood at attention. Major Harry Croel stood smiling and returned my salute. "Welcome back, Sergeant Giron," the Major said. "We thought you got lost. We were expecting you two weeks ago. The Japanese surrendered. And now you don't want to stay in the jungle anymore?" The Major ordered Sergeant Tanato to assign me to a tent.

"That's taken care of, Sir," Tanato answered and told me to throw everything in the trashcan. "You stink. Go take a shower, shave, and then go to the barbershop.

"I was saving these two shirts," Tanto continued and he handed me a fresh set of uniform. "They have their stripes still on."

"Yes," I replied. "But these are Tech Sergeant's stripes."

"That's you, Boy!" Tanato grabbed both my shoulders. "I told you I'll take care of my boys!"

I borrowed one of his trousers. I put them on without under pants, just so we could go the supply room.

Sergeant Fred Rodriguez, now also a Tech Sergeant, said, "Your pants' size is 29 waist, 26 inseam. Shirt Medium. Two Khakis, your neckties, shoes, and socks. Anything you need, just come to see me. Not the other non com OK?"

"Roger, Sarge!" I replied.

Sergeant Tanato pulled a bundle from his pocket, gave me 500 pesos. "Your pay will be here tomorrow when the pay master will come. The barber shop is there."

My hair was long for a G.I. because there is no barbershop in the jungle. The barber asked, "Straight G.I. or medium?"

Sergeant Tanato pulled out 100 pesos, gave it to the barber, winked one eye and said, "You know which one."

The barber nodded saying, "Roger, Sarge."

Officer's haircut is what I got!

"Hey Sarge…?"

But before I could open my mouth, Tanato said, "You need your money. I arranged a three-day pass for you. You'll leave tonight and be back Sunday night. Get one of my safety razor and a comb. Is that 500 pesos enough?

"It's enough." I was smiling.

Lt. Guyot was detailed to return three rented typewriters to Dagupan. My hometown is Bayambang, a town west of the highway to Dagupan. He dropped me by the riverbank then proceeded to Dagupan. I walked to the man in charge of the dug out canoes to cross the river. The Japanese had bombed the bridge, so I had to ride in the tiny canoe. While I was settling down, I asked the man how much? He looked at me for a little while, looking at my stripes, removed the homemade cigar from his mouth then cleared his throat.

"Well," he said. "Two hundred pesos, Sir."

I jumped out of the dug out and cried out, "*Two hundred pesos!?* The noise was very loud and audible, so the owner of the boat came down to the river. She spoke English.

"Can you talk to this man?" I asked. "Two hundred pesos is too much."

She and the canoe man started talking in a dialect, Pangasinan, I can understand. She introduced herself to me as the owner of the boats.

"Do you know anybody in Bayambang?" she inquired. "My name is Rosita Cayabyab." She kept looking at me. "My maiden was Rosita Pagsolingan, but I married a man by the last name of Cayabyab.

I pointed at her face, "Rosita? You're the one who was always beating me on spelling."

"And you were about to pay him 200 pesos for a canoe ride!"

She got into the boat, picked up my bag and the canoe man paddled. She was laughing.

"You never grew. You are still short."

"And you?" I retorted.

"Well, I'm a girl," she assured me. Before we alighted the boat she told me to give a pesita, 20 centavos, to the canoe man.

"How about the 200 pesos?" I asked.

"Go ahead pay if you can afford it."

I gave the old man a couple of pesetas, and we went to my uncle's house, a retired military man. Before we got there, she inquired, "Do you know these people we were about to meet?"

"Yes, he is Uncle Estanislao Millan." Rosita was already waving at the woman looking down at us from the open window. They met us at the top of the stairs.

The lady politely said, "Please enter."

Rosita quickly told the lady, "This is Leovigildo Giron, the son of Uncle Policarpo."

"Ellen's husband?" the lady asked curiously.

"Yes, I said.

Uncle Estanislao offered his hand, and I shook hands with him. Rosita gave me a side smile. She later whispered, "You forgot our customs. You were supposed to kiss his hand." My gosh, I thought, that's a long time ago.

My uncle ordered his second boy to harness the two horses while his wife was preparing to cook. My aunt assured me we have enough time before it got too dark. She opened a can of sardines. We ate in a hurry and quickly bid bye-bye. Rosita said for me to say hello to my folks. We were in a hurry. At least I was, but we can't gallop the horses because my tailbone was hurting. I never rode a horse for such a long time. On top of that my pack was bouncing up and down on my back. Finally we got to Bayambang. Home at last. Tears rolled down my cheeks.

Home At Last

The whole barrio was already dark. People turned in early to save kerosene. Dogs were barking at the sound of our horses trotting on the trail. Along side a small house, a *nipa* (palm) roofed home, we dismounted. My cousin hollered, "Nana, Nana (Auntie, Auntie) guess who is there? Somebody you know is here!"

My father quickly came down from the house and chopped down a low hanging dried coconut leaves, stripped the leaves and made a fair size torch.

My mother asked, "Who is there?"

My father lit the torch to shine light on my face.

"Who?" My mother repeated.

"Cousin *Edong*," my cousin replied, referring to me by my nickname.

My mother came close, looked closer then jerked back. "Is this my son! He is tall and big?

"He couldn't be!" my father said. "*Loco*, can't you recognize his eyes? After all it was nineteen years ago. He had to grow.

"It's him," he assured my mother (fig. 3).

I was petrified. Not a single word came out of my mouth. My tears were rolling down my cheeks. Finally my mother grabbed and hugged me. I was sobbing. The rest of the family were holding Mom's hand, the others hanging onto her skirt. The entire neighborhood was alarmed.

"What happened? Who got hurt? Is anybody sick?"

"Our brother is back," the younger girls said.

"Who?" said another sister, approaching with her sarong around her shoulders. "He is big already grown up."

My other brothers summoned my other sister. In no time at all, the entire house was full of people. I was counting my brothers and sisters who were never born when I left. This was nineteen years ago. I was 15 years old. Now I'm 34 years old. My mother was wiping my tears. I pulled my G.I. kerchief to blow my nose.

Fig. 3—Leo M. Giron and his mother in the Philippines 1973, this would be the last time Giron would be with his mother and family in the Philippines.

The older boys next to me and my two brother-in-laws went to cut down a couple of bamboo to prop the floor of the house. *It was beginning to creak.*

"My mother, my father I am home, home at last. I have missed you all so much."

In a couple of hours or so, the big wok was loaded with rice ready to cook. The pit was dug so the wok can be set for cooking. Our sisters who were married brought jars and large cans of more rice, and other spices needed for cooking. One of the brother-in-laws went and bought a marketable pig to butcher. The other brother in-law brought a few chickens. My arrival became a big great celebration. It was like the parable of the prodigal son. At the later part of the morning, I realized that I belonged to a big clan, a loving family. I have so many relatives, old and young alike. My uncle on my mother's side volunteered the use of all their chairs and benches for now the house cannot accommodate all the guests. A rich old lady across the street volunteered to use her china. There were probably 60 or 70 people, mostly kids, to feed. I told my mother and father that I think my coming home created a big imposition on all of them.

"Don't worry," my father assured me in all appeasing manner.

Mother interjected, "After all there are quite a few of us to shoulder all this."

I asked to get better reassurance, "Do we really have these many relatives?"

My mother elicited a smile. It was so unforgettable. The days of my leave went fast. I ate so much and I talked with my family. My family was so proud of me. We fought for the freedom of our country, and I was one of the lucky ones that made it. I thanked the Almighty God our Father.

Back to the Army Camp

Military routine went on and as the days went by, information was passed that those that made 70 points can be discharged from Military Service. With my Citation of a Bronze Star Medal (fig. 4), I made my 71 points. The medal was for volunteering for a secret and dangerous military intelligence mission. The citation describes the mission saying:

> He has landed by submarine in Luzon, Philippine Islands where he assisted in successfully extending lines of communication, securing vital weather data and obtaining military information which proved of the greatest assistance to impending military operations. By his loyalty, daring and skillful performance of duty under most hazardous conditions, he rendered a valuable service to operational planning and materially accelerated the campaign for recapture of the ISLANDS OF THE PHILIPPINES.
> —Signed by R.K. SUTHERLAND, Lieutenant General, United States Army, Chief of Staff

Part 2: World War II

Fig. 4—GME Giron with his Philippine Liberation Ribbon, Asiatic Pacific Campaign Medal, American Campaign Medal, World War II Victory Medal and Bronze Star Medal along with his Bronze Star Citation.

Part 3
Civilian Life & Lessons from Escrima

Back to Civilian Life

After World War II, I never thought of the art of arnis or escrima anymore. This includes the use of any firearms for that matter. I didn't see any more reason because peace in the world was finally achieved. Korean conflict, Vietnam conflict and uprising in the Philippines did not awaken my interest to renew the thought of the art of weaponry.

I got married and my number one paramount of thought was to move ahead in life after having children. I took interest in fishing as an outdoors sports but never the art of weaponry.

Then in 1966 eight nursing students were killed by a sex maniac in Chicago, and two of them were Filipino women. Eight lives were extinguished by a lunatic and not one of them made any effort to subdue the killer. They were all petrified. They could have ganged up on the man and the women would have been able to subdue him if they had the will to defend themselves. Of course this stands to reason why they were all frozen. It's apparent that they did not have any training of any kind of self-defense. Their purpose as nurses was to learn how to save lives and they were never equipped with the thought of destroying life. *If only they had a little knowledge of self defense!* This thought stayed in my mind for about a year. Why don't people ever imagine the darker part of life that might attract their interest to something about hanging onto *their* dear life?

Teaching Martial Arts Begun as a Hobby

Toward the end of 1968 I decided to open a club in Tracy, California, where I was residing at the time (fig. 1). The Veterans of Foreign Wars, which I became a member, was holding it's monthly meeting at an old jailhouse. I rented the place for the purpose of teaching the art of escrima, an effective art of self-defense.

Fig. 1—GME Giron teaching in Tracy, CA.

I use the *De Fondo* style as a base for several reasons. First, the foot movements are in harmony with another style, which I teach after the De Fondo style. Second, is the fact that this style is a close quarter defense system and that the stick is minimized to 24 inches so that the student will be forced to reduce the margin of error. This will therefore require disciplined movements of the feet, placing them at the exact or almost exact spot the Master instructs. Also, the position and angle of the stick was most effective for blocking, parrying, deflecting and evading. Third, and a very important factor to remember, is the fact that I do not teach the students to become bad. I do not teach the children to become criminals. To the contrary, the students will become more disciplined, respectful of the law and of their fellow students within the club and to anyone outside the club. They will learn to be more courteous and more considerate of others. These are the reasons why the students are never taught how to counter attack. The extent of their training is purely defensive. This concept of *strict self-defense* is at the very beginning inculcated into the minds of the students before they receive the initial movement of the art. This limitation of the mind spells out the precise meaning of the definition and the purpose of this club, hence the name "Martial Art of Self Defense."

Close Quarter Training

The *De Fondo* style has twelve numbers (fig. 2). These numbers are determined by the striking areas. Each target area is protected by various movements, and each movement is governed by existing condition at the time the strike is delivered. All in all the whole system offers one-hundred-seventy-five or more defensive movements and usually takes a minimum of two-hundred hours before the student can qualify.

What to do in order to learn this art is to abide by the daily routine. Every instructor teaches what to

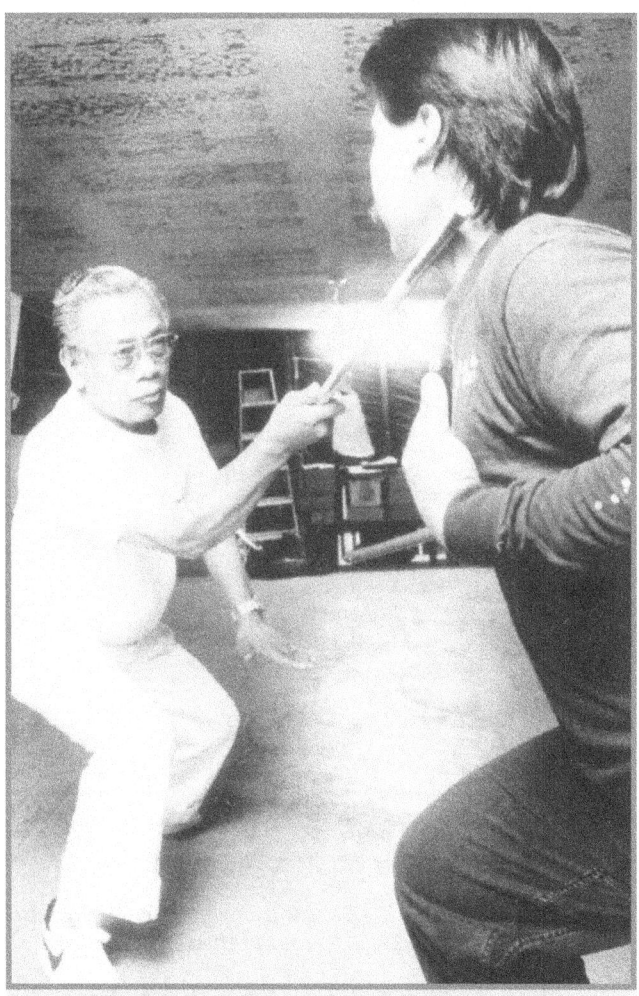

Fig. 2—GME Giron with GM Antonio Somera in Giron's basement Stockton, CA.

do. The instructor keeps the knowledge of the art within the confines of his club. He will train with his students on what to do and what not to do in combat areas. Knowing the various environments of combat situations enriches the knowledge of the student in searching for the most effective defenses.

Escrima Lessons from a Bladed Warrior
What Not To Do

If and when a problem arises between two people, try not to permit the problem to develop into a state beyond repair (fig. 3). Do not lose your balance. Do not lose your temper. Do not use words that will discomfort another person. Do not use foul words that you do not want said unto you. However, if the situation is beyond control, that physical engagement becomes inevitable, do not deliver the first blow. A good escrimador is always ready to stage the most effective self-defense.

Fig.3—GME Giron with a Tero Grave strike to GM Antonio Somera's throat in the Giron Backyard Stockton, CA 1985.

Part 3: Civilian Life & Lessons from Escrima

Justifiable Offense

Physical encounter can happen in smooth as well as in rough terrain. When terrain is smooth, there is a very good reason to assume that the encounter is taking place in a community where civil government exists. There are law enforcement officers. This slogan should be in your mind. "Don't take the law into your own hands take it to the court." But of course lawbreakers do not breed outside of civilization. Lawbreakers need victims so it may happen in communities, a small town as well as big cities. What type of criminals are these? Regardless of what they are, their criminal ventures, habitual or not, are always motivated by these four letter words: *Like-Wish-Need-Want*. I like, I wish, I need, I want. They always manage to enslave their protégés. As a result, tug-of-war begins to be more tense between these four letter words. *Good* against *Evil*, *Love* against *Hate*. The nastier of all of these is *Greed* and takes advantage of all that turns the cheek but not always to those that are alert and always on his or her guard. Finally when the situation demands, be guided by the speech of the late President Roosevelt, "Offense is the best Defense." As I may state, "This is the appropriate time to give all you got. *Bahala Na.*"

Rough Terrain

When conflict exists between good and bad, whether it takes place in smooth or rough terrain, whether it may be in big cities or in the jungle, the usual situation is that the good goes after the bad. The law after the criminal, whether a small posse after an outlaw or an army after another army. It is usually a declared war. In situations like these the careful warrior puts strong emphasis on *What Not to Do* in order to stay alive so that he can enjoy the blessings of knowing what there is to do. Let's be guided by the advise of General MacArthur to me and my group of dedicated warriors in the briefing room at the Hendorf Building in Brisbane Queensland, Australia, in August 1944 before leaving for the Philippines. I quote General MacArthur's words: "If you want to reach a ripe old age, use a little imagination, supported by a little common sense and you will live to be an old man like me."

Lessons from War

1. Do not try to be a super hero. It's better to stand proud and erect although your chest is bare of medals than to be decorated posthumously.

2. Do not go ahead of your group. Stay abreast with them. Flying bullets do not recognize your uniform from behind, especially bullets from automatic weapons.

3. Do not outrun your group believing you will find a better cover if you get there first. Careless footing can break your leg and you might not get there at all.

4. Do not think the next foxhole is safer than yours. You might get mowed down before you get to the next one.

5. When on sniper mission do not use or carry anything that glitters that might give you away.

6. Do not be too eager to hit your second target lest you will be spotted soon.

7. Do not load the chamber of your rifle more than one round at a time. Reload your piece slow and easy and catch your empty shells. Keep them in your pocket if you are on a tree. The empty shells will give you away.

8. Do not make sudden moves that are not as natural as the prevailing wind. If you do, you might never move again.

9. Do not make trails leading to your sniper's nest. It's a give away.

10. Do not panic if you get injured. You should be equipped properly with a first aid kit and know how to use it.

11. During night operation and encounter avoid shooting lest you hit your own comrades. Use your bolo or bayonet.

12. Do not fight the war by yourself. Always belong to a team and help each other.

13. Do not be too eager to pick a souvenir. It might be rigged for a booby trap.

14. When trailing small patrols, do not be fooled by the footprints. Observe also the direction the grass is bent. That's where the patrol went. They might deliberately walk backward to deceive you.

Part 3: Civilian Life & Lessons from Escrima

15. Do not trust civilian guides especially when they walk too far ahead of your group. They might lead you to an ambush.

16. Do not walk blindly in the jungle. Investigate hanging leaves or branches on your trail especially from foot to head elevation. There might be trip vine for a booby trap snare.

17. Always remember how many and who are the civilians traveling with you. You want to know why all of a sudden one is missing, or one or two were added to the group.

18. If you have been operating in an area long enough to know the trails, do not fail to understand the reason for the sudden noise and flight of birds. If you are passing through and you are a familiar sight to them, they simply fly away from the trail and then come back to look for food without making alarming noises. Dogs also bark more intently when unfamiliar persons and smells come by.

19. If you see smoke arising amidst a grove of trees, do not fail to listen for dogs barking or cock crowing at dawn. If these sounds are not present, it is a temporary camp. It could be your enemy.

20. When you want to avoid molestation of the girls, the Japanese are very particular about having contact with girls with (TB) tuberculosis of the lung.

21. Unless you want to aggravate a Japanese soldier, never call him "DOROBO." This means bandit. He will charge *bansai* right away.

23. Never salute or call your officer "Sir." He is the favorite target of the sniper.

24. Even if all your comrades are all good buddies, it's been known that men under tremendous pressure will change to a beast. He might cut your throat over a simple souvenir.

Lessons from Life

Let these guide you to a bit of common sense that you may be able to use in life.

1. Do not let your enemy know that you are afraid of him. Remember, he is also afraid of you. Once you allow fear to get the best of you, your fighting spirit hence your power is gone. Act superior but be careful.

2. Act defensively and do not take chances. Even cats with nine lives die but once.

3. Do not open your mouth unnecessarily. The fish was fried in hot oil because he opened his mouth.

4. Listen while you can. The last word of advice might be the word to save you.

5. Do not remove your shoes when crossing a shallow river or creek. You might step on a sharp pointed object purposely placed by the enemy.

6. When engaged in bolo combat, when the terrain is not level, endeavor to place yourself on the lower elevation looking up to your opponent. Picture yourself on the upper position bending forward and downward to reach your opponent. Visualize yourself retreating backward and upward at the same time.

7. When your opponent is charging or assaulting downward, you will be a low profiled target from his point of view especially when you are hugging the ground ready to launch at him.

8. If you are assaulting the enemy on a downgrade and he is well emplaced, circle around to obtain an equal elevation. You will have an equal chance to use your skill in combat.

9. When vegetation is abundant and shrubs and bushes are plentiful, avoid wild swinging angular or horizontal. Your weapon can be apprehended by vines or branches and your timing will be impaired. You chance the risk of being injured or killed.

10. When using your bolo, do not jump around in the dark. If you trip or fall, it's hard to get up while under pressure.

11. Do not crowd your neighbor so that each of you can use your full potential without accidentally hitting each other.

12. Do not go to a fight without a secondary weapon. You might break your only bolo.

13. Do not engage in combat with a heavy pack. If you have time, remove it so you can move more freely.

14. Do not straddle a log lying on the ground. Place one foot on it then jump away because a cobra might be coiled ready to strike on the opposite side.

15. Do not give food to only one or two out of a group of hungry children unless you have enough for all of them. They will kill the one's with food.

16. If you are looking for a stream or creek for water, don't go looking where there are no green shrubs and trees. This foliage thrives on water and usually grows along the creek.

17. When engaged in a bolo knife combat, do not try to chop down your foe with one blow. A light snap at the fleshy part of the body especially on muscles will cut to the bone, assuming your bolo is sharp. To cut across the bone hoping to sever the portion of the body is taking a chance of breaking your bolo. If it does not break, chances are that the bolo will get stuck and since a dying man does not always fall down to your favor, you might not recover your bolo on time.

It is the purpose of the author to mention the many *lessons* of life and war as he experienced. They are the *don'ts* of life and war. He is sure there are many more situations to avoid especially in other theaters of operation. By knowing these *don'ts* and how to avoid them can provide the extension of ones precious life. The things to do will come easy as one goes along through training, through the borrowed experience of those that lived long enough to tell and foremost by understanding various situations as may be suggested by existing conditions and circumstances. It is a common slogan in civilian life to "live and learn." In war one must "learn and live."

The author, now in his declining years at 80 is still teaching the art of escrima for a hobby after retiring from Federal service of 30 year's long.

Part 4
History of the Filipino Lodge

Many Filipino American historians would claim that during the early days of Filipinos in America, Filipino clubs, associations, organizations and lodges would be a unique feature of Filipino American society. Most of these organizations of Filipinos would be governed by a Constitution and set of By-laws. They would be governed by members who would elect officers to achieve specific goals. They would build social ties, character, promote and protect the groups' interests, build unity among members and other social groups. They would promote and encourage community and social events, social activities, and participate in historical secret rituals to preserve the teachings of Filipino national heroes who were responsible for the fight for independence and freedom of the Philippines. They would promote social and economic equality amongst all men and women. They would help in the fight for social equality and to basically help each other to become better citizens in their newly found country, the United States of America. They would carry out the mission of Brotherhood and establish fraternity among the laborers in the working class.

During the period of the first wave of Filipinos coming to America from 1906 to 1934, Filipinos would find themselves working in less than adequate working conditions and forced to take jobs that no one person would want to take. They would do backbreaking "stoop labor" by working in the fields and farmlands of America (fig. 1). These young "Pinoys," as the young Filipino

Fig. 1—Filipino farm workers cutting asparagus in the Islands of the San Joaquin Valley of California.

men called themselves, would be promised greater opportunities in a new land, where they could find their fame and fortune. Instead their destiny led to signing a biding contract to work in labor camps in America. Waking up before dawn to work in the fields of itchy peat dirt during the sunny summer heat, with temperatures that could reach over 100 degrees and muddy fields soaked with rain in the cold winter in less than 40 degree temperatures. When Filipinos left their families and friends in the Philippines, they had no dreams of returning to their native homeland. Most Filipinos were never to see their families and friends again. They would work long hard days for pennies an hour. Many of these Pinoys would face racial discrimination along with verbal and physical abuse from many of the local white citizens.

In order to fill their need for social contact that was free from racial discrimination, Pinoys would search out other groups of Pinoys. Many Pinoys would know of a friend or "town mate" that may already belong to a Filipino organization, and they would join to be connected to this safe and secure social group. This was how Pinoys would survive during these trying times filled with an unstable climate of racial tension.

The "BIG THREE" **Secret Filipino Fraternal Orders,** as many Filipinos would refer to them, were the Caballeros de Dimas Alang, Grand Oriente Filipino and the strongest and most powerful Legionarios del Trabajo. All these social groups were transplants from the Philippines. Members of the Cabaleros de Dimas Alang took their pen name "Dimas Alang" from the Philippine national hero and patriot Dr. Jose Rizal. Cabaleros de Dimas Alang was established in America in 1920 in San Francisco and would grow to the strength of more that two thousand men and women with one hundred lodges and included many women's circles. Grand Oriente Filipino, in mix translation means "Great Filipino Lodge." Grand Oriente Filipino also started in 1920 in San Francisco. Grand Oriente grew to the strength of over seven hundred men and one hundred women. The last of the "BIG THREE" was and still is one of the most powerful Filipino Lodges. Legionarios del Trabajo of America Inc. translates to "Legionnaires of Labor." The first lodge was started in America in 1924 also in San Francisco. Membership would peak at over three thousand Filipinos with 86 lodges that include twelve lodges for women. Grand Master Emeritus Leo M. Giron (fig. 2) along with my father Chester Serna Somera Sr., my brother Chester Celestino Somera Jr., and I would belong to the Legionarios del Trabajo, Lodge name General Luna #602 (fig 3). These lodges were packed and filled with many first-generation immigrant Pinoys, forty percent served our country during World War II and all of them had the working knowledge of *Arnis Escrima*. All the members were known to me as "uncle" or "auntie" out of respect of my father's connection with the lodge. And many of them would open the door to me about the style of Arnis Escrima they would play. This would be one of the Legionarios del Trabajo's living treasures and one great opportunity to learn more about my Filipino history and culture. Because of Grand Master Emeritus Leo M. Giron and my family being members of the Legionarios del Trabajo, the following will be a brief history as told to me by Illustrious Brother Bart R. Navarro past Grand

Fig. 2—Supreme Minister Ill. Bro. Leo M. Giron of the LDT.

Master and Illustrious Brother Leo M. Giron past Sovereign Minister.

History of the Legionarios del Trabajo

From the earliest account there were two groups unknown to each other that were active and very much involved in the propagation and expansion of the Fraternity in San Francisco. One group was led by Ill. (Illustrious) Bro. (Brother) Norberto Villanueva who obtained light from the "Trece de Agosto Lodge" in Manila, Philippines. The other group was headed by Ill. Bro. Pedro Ponce—his relationship to Ill. Bro. Domingo Ponce Founder of the Legionarios del Trabajo was not established. From Ill. Bro. Gerardo Borja's account, this latter group initiated their new members in the apartment occupied by Bro. Manahan on the third week of April 1924 (fig. 4). Realizing that unity and not duplicity was of the essence to achieve their purpose, the two groups got together, and a joint meeting was held at the California Hall on June 24, 1924, in San Francisco. Five days later, on June 29, 1924, another meeting was held and the groups elected their first permanent officers and adopted their By-Law. Appropriately, the lodge was named "Mayon Lodge" in admiration of the Mayon Volcano in the Philippines and also because it symbolizes Light and Solidarity that would propagate the principles and doctrines of the Legionarios. The Mayon Lodge #459 was registered in San Francisco and Bro. Paciano Sanchez served as the first Worshipful master.

After six months of tutoring and guiding the new lodge, Ill. Bro. Pedro Ponce, who had played a major part in the initial phase, decided to go back to the Philippines. On December 26, 1924 at a farewell banquet held in his honor at the Paradise Inn in San Francisco, he remarked:

> I have traveled ten thousand miles from home to come to this land of opportunity with one purpose in view: that my people may be enlightened with the principles and teachings of the

Fig. 3—L to R, Ill. Bro. Chester C. Somera Jr., Ill. Bro. Chester S. Somera Sr., Bro Antonio E. Somera, all members of the General Luna Lodge #602.

Part 4: History of the Filipino Lodge

Fig. 4—Birthplace of the Legionarios del Trabajo in America. 625 Polk Street, California Hall, San Francisco, California.

Legionarios del Trabajo. I have sown the seeds. Now it is up to you to continue so that our people may share the light and glory of Brotherhood.

The die was cast. It was not in vain and the seed grew!

There was sufficient potential for expansion. Many more Filipinos were arriving from the Philippines due to unlimited entry and there was no quota restriction for immigration to the United States. The new arrivals were mostly single men, and if they were married, their wives were left behind. Because of the limited number of Filipino women from their country, Pinoy social life was minimal but racial tension in the new land was high. Ill. Bro. Norberto Villanueva wrote about his "ten registrants" having meetings nightly after work, because they could not go to the movies, a vaudeville

Fig. 5—First Annual Public Installation of Worshipful Daguhoy Lodge #528, January 6, 1934.

show, or the zoo for relaxation and enjoyment. There had to be an outlet from a socially isolated existence and joining an organization provided this. It was for their best interest. The three organizations—namely, the Legionarios del Trabajo in America, the Caballeros de Dimas Along, and the Filipino Federation of America—were waiting in the wings.

In 1925 the Kalapati Lodge #515 of Oakland and the Noli Me Tangere Lodge #516 of Berkeley were organized. These two lodges, with the Mayon Lodge #459, formed the nucleus of the Supreme Regional Council. The authority for the Supreme Regional Council was to establish and also appoint Ill. Bro. Norberto Villanueva as Grand Delegate. The order was contained in a letter dated August 25, 1925, from Ill. Bro. Jose C. Hilario, the current Grand Secretary of the Grand General Assemble of Manila. At the first Annual Convention held on December 2-3, 1926, the Supreme Regional Council was reorganized and it became the Supreme Fraternal council of the Legionarios del Trabajo in America. Ill. Bro. Norberto

Villanueva had the honor to be the first elected Grand Delegate in the history of the Fraternity.

Three more lodges were organized in 1927. They were Bisig Lodge #527 of San Mateo, Daguhoy Lodge #528 of Stockton (fig. 5) with Bro. Cruz Ranario the first Worshipful Master, and Los Angeles Lodge #529 of Los Angles California. Stockton had the largest Filipino population in American, and because of this it was nicknamed "Little Manila." Currently the Daguhoy lodge #528 of Stockton, California is still registered and active with the Grand Lodge of the Legionarios del Trabajo in America.

Before completing his term of office, Ill. Bro. Norberto Villanueva resigned on September 19, 1927. Ill. Bro. Gerardo Borja was appointed to take his place. During the term of Ill. Bro Gerardo Borja there were five more lodges chartered.

In 1929 Ill. Bro. Hugo Castaneda had taken on the responsibility of Grand Delegate. During Ill. Bro. Hugo Castaneda's short term there was one more lodge chartered, the Liwanag Lodge #540 of Long Beach California. In 1930 Ill. Bro. Antonio Jusay was elected the Grand Delegate. The Circle of the Truth and Chamber of the Nobles were organized but became dormant because of lack of membership. It must be noted that the last three years did not produce as many lodges as expected. It was not a question of leadership ineptness but rather to the prevailing economic conditions: These were the Great Depression years. There were no jobs and no money to spend. Mobility was limited. In one sense, it was a good thing because it gave the new lodges time to consolidate their gains and to make plans for the future.

From 1931 through 1936, Ill. Bro. Benito I. Falcon served as the Grand Delegate. During this time there were seven more lodge's chartered. This included a women's only lodge from Stockton, Teodora Alonzo Lodge #123. Sis. Albina Pasco served as the first Worthy Matron and among the seven lodges that were formed was the powerful General Luna Lodge #602 of Lodi. Bro. Florencio V. Bautista would be the first Worshipful Master. It is noted that the General Luna Lodge #602 produced one of the highest number of Grand Masters to serve the Grand Lodge. It is also noted that Leo M. Giron and Chester Serna Somera (Antonio E. Somera's Father) would serve the General Luna lodge their entire life.

There were two outstanding features of this administration. The first feature was the initial effort of the Legionarios del Trabajo in America to organize women lodges. The second is the formation of the Daguhoy Band, which became the pride and joy of the Fraternity. The band participated in many Independence and Armed forces Day parades in many communities in California. It also performed during the Grand Convention, the last one in 1951 in Sacramento. The effect of their participation was a positive projection of the Filipino community in the eyes of the American people.

Between the years of 1937 to 1940, Ill. Bro. Roque E el la Ysla served as the Grand Delegate. His term of office witnessed a phenomenal growth of the Fraternity. With the outbreak of World War II, many Filipino's joined the US Army to win back their Philippine homeland. Jobs became plentiful in agricultural and industrial areas. There was money to be spent. Filipinos flocked to work in the fields and the rich farmlands throughout the state of California. What remained was to organize these Filipinos and to bring them into the fold of the Brotherhood. The members of the Order worked diligently in recruiting members and the number of lodges organized. There were twenty new lodges chartered. besides the large number of converts to the causes of the Fraternity. Ill Bro. Goque E. de la Ysla is to be remembered for finalizing and registering the Incorporation Papers of the Fraternity on June 24, 1937, with the office of the Secretary of State in Sacramento.

Ill. Bro. Antonio Cruz followed as Grand Delegate in 1941 through 1943. The war in Europe and the Pacific became more intense and severe, but it did not distract the Order from bringing in more members. During this time another nine lodges were chartered. This included General Lim Lodge #627, where Bro. Veancio Baltazar became the first Worshipful Master. In this lodge Ill. Bro. Joe Papaco and Ill. Bro Victorino Ton were both well known to lodge members as great masters of the art of Escrima Arnis. Note that both Manong Pacpaco and Manong Ton were both members of Bahala Na Martial Arts Association. Manong Joe Pacpaco is currently 97 years old and living in Stockton and Manong Victorino Ton lived to be 108 years old, living through three centuries.

Ill. Bro. Felipe M. Esteban was elected Grand Delegate between the years 1944 through 1949 and was also Grand Master between the years 1952 through 1953. During his incumbency of eight years, eighteen more lodges were founded. When World War II came to a close, members of the Armed Forces came back to the continental United States. Upon arrival Filipinos started to arrange for their wives to come to the America—this was mainly because of their status as American Soldiers. And many more Filipinos applied and received their citizenship status. They were also able to bring relatives to America. Many of these members would be allowed to marry and then would join the Fraternity. The conclusion of the Korean War brought the same condition.

The efforts to have more Filipinos to join the Fraternity reached its peak during Esteban's administration. With this unprecedented response for membership was also a concerted effort to buy some real estate for future use of the Fraternity. This farsighted and long range planning paid off. Through a loan subscription from the members, there was enough money raised which was used to purchase 160 acres of farmland in Lathrop. The land was purchased for $35,000, and now this piece of property is worth millions in the present real estate market.

Likewise, the administration of Ill. Bro. Felipe M. Esteban is credited for starting the Queen Contest that is now an established tradition during the Grand Convention. The coronation of the fairest is the social highlight of the weeklong affair. Of great importance is that the money raised from this project has been distributed in the form of Scholarship Awards to deserving young people associated with the Fraternity.

Ill. Bro. Bart R. Navarro served two years both as Grand Delegate and Grand Master. From 1950 through 1951, there were ten more lodges organized. The outstanding phase of Ill. Bro. Bart R. Navarro's administration is the emergence and formulation of the Educational System that form the heart of the Rites and Dogmas, as well as the Practical, Symbolic, and Parabolic teachings of the Fraternity. Navarro saw the necessity for some readjustments in America. Through a Plebiscite that was overwhelmingly approved by the Lodges in America, he was able to get a sanction from Ill. Bro. Doming Ponce for the establishment of a Supreme Consistory in America. This change in the spiritual hierarchy was accomplished in 1951. The Supreme Fraternal Council established in 1926 under Ill. Bro. Norberto Villanueva was terminated, and the title Grand Delegate became the title of Grand Master. The Legionarios del Trabajo in America owes Ill. Bro. Bart R. Navarro sincere gratitude for his contribution in this sensitive field. The late Ill. Bro. Domingo Ponce admitted and confided that the educational system in America, when compared with the Philippines, was far better, more advanced, and more realistic. It was also during his term of office that the Drum and Bugle Corps was organized, which participated in many parades in different communities in California.

From 1954 through 1957, Ill. Bro. Luciano P. Blas held the office of Grand Master. The drive for membership continued and was successful on the distaff side. During the administration of Ill. Bro. Blas three men's lodges were formed and five women's lodges were also formed. His term of office found five woman lodges organized. The influx of women from the Philippines, either as wives of ex-servicemen, relatives, students, tourists, or whether under some arrangement with the government continued. Before the time limit expired on their stay in the United States, many Filipino women found it expedient to get married to American citizens of Filipino descent. This was indeed a blessing to the Legionarios del Trabajo in America because many joined the Fraternity with their husbands.

Ill. Bro. Luciano P. Blas is also remembered for adherence and observance of practical instructions during meetings. The sublime Circle of the Truth was reactivated and Ill. Bro. Glicerio Mariano was elected as Grand Chancellor. He was also responsible for acquisition of the house adjoining the Legionarios building. This was now called the "White House," because at that time it would only be reserved for the Grand Master to occupy the residence during meetings, conventions or if the Grand Master chose to live there, but during Ill. Bro. Blas's term, it was utilized as the central office of the Legionarios.

In 1958 until 1959, Ill. Bro. Eddie B. Olamit Sr. followed as Grand Master. Two more women lodges were organized.

Many brothers and sisters got married and have raised families. The numbers of their offsprings have grown, and there was a desire to orient them with the elementary teachings of the Fraternity. It was during Olamit's administration when the Junior Lodges came into being. Ill. Bro conceived the idea with Pedro A Adlao, a schoolteacher, who is very much interested in the affairs of young people. On July 6 and 7, 1972, the first annual conference of the group was held at Edison High School in Stockton. Five lodges were represented and led by their commanders. The five Junior Lodges that participated were: Junior Lodge #1 of Stockton (headed by Bart R. NavarroJr.), Junior Lodge #2 of Livingston (headed by Luna Jamero), Junior Lodge #3 of Salinas (headed by Juanita Narciso), Junior Lodge #4 of San Jose (headed by Arthur Barreras), and Junior Lodge #5 of Delano was headed by Pacienca Blas. The Junior Lodges were successful and Sister Eleanor Olamit of the Teodora Alonzo Lodge #123 of Stockton, California led the conference facilitating its great success.

From 1960 to 1961, Ill. Bro. Modesto Buenviaje succeeded as Grand Master and one more womens lodge was organized. His term of office has the distinction of initiating the "Pro-Rata" system, in which the unpaid hospital claims that were of sizable amount was liquidated slowly to the satisfaction of the Fraternity.

From 1962 through 1975 Ill, Bro. Antonio T. Santos holds office of Grand Master. The addition of one more men's lodge and five women lodges were organized. The five women's lodges is significant because these lodges are now developing into a potent force that will exert plenty of influence in the future affairs of the Fraternity. Between 1958 through 1975, of the ten lodges organized, nine were women and only one for men. The other seven women lodges organized before 1958 are attracting and increasing their membership. The feeling of the elders in the lodge is that the women are the key to a stronger and better Legionarios del Trabajo in America. The omens are all present. Women are now appointed to the higher level of committee assignments. Lately, some have been elected to various offices in the Grand Lodge. Who could deny that the Fraternity is the strongest exponent of Women's Liberation!

During the early stages of Ill. Bro. Santo's administration, the Fraternity was beset with cumbersome and duplicated lines of authority. The Grand Master could not function effectively under this condition. The Council of Fifteen, an elective body established in Los Angeles in 1960, was eliminated and replaced by an appointive body known as the Council of Elders. It was later change into the Advisory Council consisting of five members. In 1964, the Constitution and By-Laws was amended and vested the Spiritual Power in the Supreme Consistory. The Grand Patriarch, its highest officer, was made co-equal with the office of the Grand Master. This arrangement deprived and took the ceremonial duties from the Grand Master and became a divisive factor in the Fraternity. The constitution Study Committee appointed in 1967 remedied the dilemma. On February 21, 1970, after three years of in-depth study of the Constitution and By-Laws, the Grand Assembly adopted the recommendation that the Grand Master is the source of all power and must not be shared with any other officer. The title of Grand Patriarch was changed to Sovereign Minister who "may exercise certain independence, but he or she must work hand in hand with the Grand Master" but not as co-equal. The late Ill. Bro. Felipe M. Esteban was the first and only Grand Patriarch, and Ill. Bro. Leo M. Giron was chosen as the new Sovereign Minister.

The Judicial System underwent some changes. The Board of Review was erased from the books and the functions transferred and absorbed by other bodies. The sub-divisions, formerly know as Regions, were redefined with added responsibilities. They are now called Councils and are functioning under strict guidelines set up by the Grand Lodge. The office of Vice Grand Master was created, followed by the addition of the 2nd Vice Grand Master. These organizational reforms were essential to meet the demands and pressures of the complexities of administration.

Considered to be one of the most notable pieces of legislation was the granting to all members in the Master Degree the right to be delegates and be able to vote for the candidates for the various grand offices during the Grand Convention. The extension of this right and franchise opened and democratized the Fraternity. It has motivated greater interest and increased participation in the decision making process.

After many years of frustration, on November 1964, members saw the completion and dedication of the Legionarios del Trabajo in American Building located at 2154 South San Joaquin Street, Stockton. On this day a beautiful dream came true to all Legionarios. The Patience of the members who paid twelve dollars each for ten years, and who continue to make financial donations of varying amounts, is significant. Efforts of the lodges that bought and donated furniture cannot be overlooked. Surely, this was a team effort.

Perhaps the most momentous event in the history of the Legionarios del Trabajo in America was the winning of her independence. The Fait Accompli occurred in 1965 when Ill. Bro. Antonio T. Santos Grand Master and Ill. Bro. Ray A. Cabanilla (Grand Secretary) journeyed ten thousand miles to attend the Grand Convention in Manila. The journey was very fruitful. In a series of conferences with Ill. Bro. Domingo Ponce, Founder and Supreme Head of the Legionarios Del Trabajo, Ill Bro. Santos and Ill. Bro Cabanilla were able to obtain from Ill. Bro. Domingo Ponce his signature to a "Document of Separation and Consent" that made the Legionarios del Trabajo in America separate, sovereign, and equal with the Supreme Consistory in Manila. Obtaining this autonomous status meant that the Order in America can chart its own course, work independently without interference, and be the master of her own destiny. There was no compensation or proviso in the agreement for division of assents, but it was accomplished in the best tradition of good will and cordiality. For this benevolent gesture, Ill. Bro. Domingo Ponce deserves the highest admiration and gratitude of all Legionarios throughout the world. The Legionarios del Trabajo in America found a new sense of direction.

As indicated in Ill. Bro. Antonio T. Santos' message in the Souvenir Program in 1964, his administration is also committed to a "constructive youth program vital to the future of our Fraternity and this country." In good faith with the commitment, commencing in 1966, part of the proceeds derived from the Queen Contest, is distributed in the form of Scholarship Awards to deserving kin of Legionario members. These awards, together with the Life Membership diplomas to loyal and devoted members who have 30 years continuous membership or accumulated 35 years of active membership, are given at the Annual Dinner and Dance on Saturday following the Grand Assembly.

Culturally and on the aesthetic side, Ill. Bro. Antonio T. Santos and the First Lady, Ill. Sister Mickey Santos, have donated a mural, in the name of the Grand Lodge, to the City of Stockton. A mural also adorns the Grand Assembly Hall of the Legionarios del Trabajo in America Building. The two murals are the works of Bro. Greg Custodio, a talented artist and member of the Mabini Lodge #610.

Although the Order is non-political, the Legionarios del Trabajo in America included, among their guests during Grand Assemblies and Grand Conventions, names that are well known in the political and diplomatic fields. This is indicative and a realization of the growing power of the Fraternity in local, state, and national level. Who could tell that someday a Legionarios will distinguish them for public service whether it is elective or appointive?

In 1968, to allay any fears of legal entanglements, the Incorporation Papers were reviewed, revised, and up-dated to meet the requirements for philanthropic organizations as provided by the statues of the State of California. A copy of this legal document is registered at the Office of the Secretary of State in the City of Sacramento, California.

The struggle for existence and survival of the Legionarios del Trabajo in America was not a picnic. The early pioneers of the movement experienced some sad and distasteful incidents in their quest for membership. The hardships and sacrifices brought by discriminatory hang-ups were raw. These faults and shortcoming are human failings that must be tolerated with understanding and compassion. However, these unfortunate outside distractions provided a true test of the fabric and character that a Legionarios possesses. Indeed, he was equal to the task. He did not falter but succeeded. Nations and people fight to maintain or extend their geographical frontiers. The frontier of the Legionarios del Trabajo in America is reaching men and women's hearts so they could dwell in unity in the true spirit of Brotherhood and Sisterhood.

Currently the Legionarios del Trabajo in America is still an active force and entity that follows the rituals and ceremonies of our founding Fathers. In some respects it is a secret society that values and respects the rights of common labor and citizens. It helps Filipinos build their own self-confidence, of learning knowledge and freedom for all. It could be said that the traditional ancient rituals and ancient ceremonies fall along the lines of a secret society: Of patriots maybe even the Katipunan and that these ancient rituals and ancient ceremonies that were practiced over a hundred years ago are still practiced to this day. If you dare to search for light of history and Filipino culture at its very best seek out one of the greatest Filipino Fraternal Orders in our lifetime. Look no further, you will find it within The Legionarios del Trabajo in America.

Francisco Daguhoy

During the 330 years of occupation of Spain in the Philippines, there were many revolts and rebellions, but one in particular was a rebellion in Bohol by a Filipino patriot Francisco Daguhoy. After Tamblot's revolt in 1621, Bohol went through more than a century of comparative peace. Throughout this period, however, the Spaniards made no effort to reform their despotic colonial rule. In 1774, a man by the name of Francisco Daguhoy was enraged by the refusal of a Jesuit curate to bury his brother who died in the service of the church. Daguhoy took advantage of the occasion to arouse the long pent-up resentment of the Boholanos against the Spaniards and rallied 3,000 Boholanos to his side.

After harassing and inflicting several defeats on the Spanish forces, Daguhoy triumphantly announced the independence of Bohol. For 85 years thereafter, the Boholanos were able to maintain their independence by repelling all Spanish attempts to retake the island. According to the historian Gregorio F. Zaide, the following factors contributed to Daguhoy's success.

First, the fierce determination and fighting prowess of the Boholano patriots that had recorded engaging battles using long weapons against the Spanish, even though the Spanish would recruit Filipino soldiers. Second, the decadence of the Spanish regime as shown by the fact that the Spaniards of the period were no longer consummate fighters like the early conquistadores; again the Spanish would recruit the more experienced Filipino fighters. Third, the raging Moro wars that sapped the strength of the Spaniards in the Philippines and distracted the attention of the Spanish authorities.

During Daguhoy's reign, the Spanish authorities both political and ecclesiastical officials, made overtures to pacify him but all of these failed. Even an expedition under Don Pedro Lechuga was beaten back by the rebel forces. After Daguhoy's death, his subordinate leaders carried on the struggle to preserve their hard-earned liberty.

The "Daguhoy Lodge No. 528, was named in honor of Francisco Daguhoy, leader of the Boholanos, who established a native government and lived as independent people for one hundred years. The Daguhoy Lodge was organized on December 26, 1926, and a charter issued on February 11, 1927. This Lodge is one of the first to be established in America to carry out the teachings of the Legionarios del Trabajo.

During the administration of General del la Torre, Daguhoy led an insurrection destined to become famous and to occupy a brilliant page in the annals of Philippine history. As in the case of most revolts, and because of the Filipinos' inborn love of liberty, this was in protest of the abuses and oppression of the Spanish government and the friars.

Daguhoy Filipino Lodge

Today, located in the Historic Downtown Little Manila District of Stockton California is the Daguhoy Filipino Lodge. The Daguhoy Lodge #528, Legionarios Del Trabajo In America is the first Lodge owned and operated by its members in the Legionarios Del Trabajo in the United States. Named in honor of Francisco Daguhoy, a Boholano who led a successful rebellion in the province of Bohol against Spanish authorities, the Lodge was organized on the second Sunday in October 1926, at the Eagle's Hall in Stockton, California. On the second Sunday in November 1926, a constitution and by-laws were adopted and the election of officers held. The original fourteen members pursued a charter from the Sobernao National Consistorio del Trabajo, Manila, Islas Filipinas, which was approved on February 11, 1927 with the numerical designation of "528," legally recognizing its establishment in the City of Stockton, County of San Joaquin, California, U.S.A. This Lodge was then pivotal in the organization of the subsequent Lodges formed in the San Joaquin Valley.

It was decided that the Lodge should purchase a permanent home for its membership and to serve as a meeting place for Filipinos living in the area. Having a meeting place for the Filipino community was particularly important as there were few places in Stockton, aside from the taxi dance halls, pool rooms, and bars, where Filipino families could come together to socialize (fig. 6). Purchasing a facility, however, was difficult because of the

Fig. 6—Annual Convention of the "Legionarios del Trabajo de Filipinas, February 6 & 7, 1932.

several laws that impeded the progress of ownership of land at the time. The Alien Land Act of 1913 prohibited the sale of land to Asian Pacific Islanders who were not born in the United States. Most Filipino born in the Philippines were considered Wards of the United States and ineligible for citizenship. In addition, there was intense racial discrimination and antagonism in the 1930s and 1940s toward Filipinos and other minorities.

Despite these barriers, the Daguhoy Lodge became a reality with the purchase of the property and building for sixteen thousand dollars at 203 East Hazelton Avenue. A Deed of Trust was dated December 27, 1937 and executed by Antonio R. Cruz to Security Title Insurance and Guarantee Company and consummated on January 17, 1938. The property was later transferred to three Lodge officers by a decree of quitting title on July 13, 1950, with the Deed transferred to Daguhoy Lodge on March 16, 1961.

The Daguhoy Lodge #528, L.D.T. has been the meeting place for individuals, families, and Filipino organizations from its beginning and continues to serve that purpose today (fig. 7). As its membership grew and the need for additional meeting space increased, several building projects were planned and completed in the 1930s and 1940s, including a temple structure, large kitchen, and porch.

Fig. 7—Legionarios del Trabajo wedding ceremony of Brother Chester S. Somera Sr. & Sister Frances M. Cunningham at the Stockton Civic Auditorium, April 1, 1954.

Although not architecturally significant, its history has deep roots in the Filipino community and the Stockton area. In the beginning, the building lodged and provided meals to Lodge members who worked as farm laborers, helping to increase membership because housing was very limited. The Lodge organized numerous activities for the community and the Brass Band that participated in many community activities including the fourth of July parades, Captain Weber's Day parades, Armistice Day parades, Salinas Big Week parades, Lodi Grape Festival and national Wine Show, Rio vista Bass Derby, and many more (fig 8). The site was a place where sports activities such as volleyball were played. In addition, the Lodge funded presents for children at a Christmas party, provided scholarships, and gave awards during commencements at local high schools (fig 9).

Fig. 8—Daguhoy Concert Band performance during the Rizal Day Commemoration held in Stockton, California at the Stockton Civic Auditorium, December 30, 1937.

Fig. 9—Legionarios in a 1947 Buick Convertible during the Stockton July 4, 1952 parade downtown Stockton, California.

Daguhoy Filipino Museum

Recently, Tony Somera, a board member of the Little Manila Foundation, Daguhoy Filipino Lodge member and Grand Master of the Bahala Na Martial Arts Association, discovered the vast treasures now held in the museum collection while doing some cleaning at the lodge during the transition of the Bahala Na Filipino Martial Arts Association from their training club located in North Stockton to South Stockton (fig. 10). Over the years many people had lived at the lodge. Stored in the basement, and almost forgotten, were years of personal mementos left behind as the fortunes of life fluctuated. There were pictures (fig. 11), posters, newspapers, magazines, personal and group photos, musical scores, poetry, essays, letters and even books of jokes that were written by the manongs (elders). There were beds, tables and chairs from the period (fig. 12). There were receipts and ledgers from small businesses of the time. There were zoot suits, clothes, watches, lighters and other personal items. Tony even found a hand forged sword, spear and shield! Some of the most striking items are the many military medals, memorabilia and uniforms that were left behind as the heroic Filipino American soldiers, who fought for our country in WWII, moved on to continue their normal lives. These World War II veterans were from the world famous and highly decorated 1st and 2nd Filipino Infantry along with General Douglas MacArthur's 978th Signal Crop. They were the first known commandos of their caliber during World War II history. Somera during his research of many of the items uncovered the fact that Filipino Martial Art icon Juan LaCoste was shot and killed at the Daguhoy Lodge. 108-year-old Victorino Ton who lived at the Daguhoy Lodge was the oldest Filipino of the Lodge. Manong Ton was a member of the Bahala Na Martial Arts Association an honorary Bahala Na Guro and life member of the Daguhoy Lodge (fig. 13).

Fig. 10— Bahala Na Martial Arts Association and Little Manila Foundation Christmas luncheon at the Daguhoy Lodge, December 3, 2005.

Part 4: History of the Filipino Lodge

Fig. 11—This is a section of the Daguhoy Filipino Museum located at the Daguhoy Lodge Stockton, California. Currently over 1,000 Filipino artifacts dating from the 1920's to 1970's.

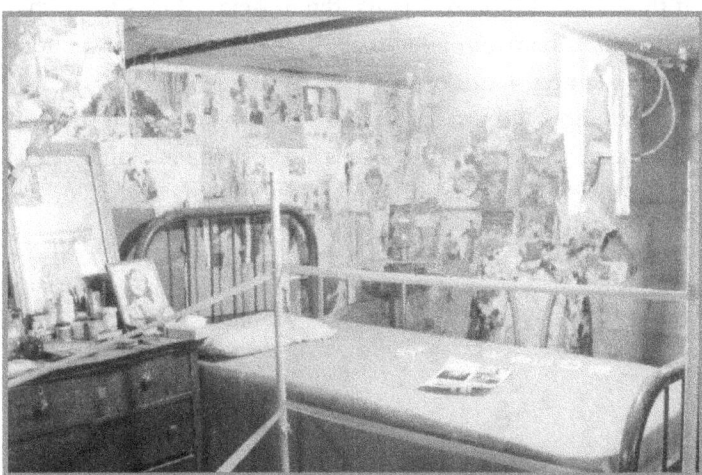

Fig. 12—In the Daguhoy Filipino Museum, an original bedroom setting with pictures torn from 1930's magazines glued to the walls by the first Manong's that arrive from the Philippines.

Fig. 13—L to R, GME Leo M. Giron at 88 years old, GM Antonio Somera and Master Victorino Ton at the age of 106 still living at the Daguhoy Lodge.

Tony Somera renovated the space and put the collected materials in order for viewing. He created a museum space that approximates the living conditions of the time being displayed along with unique and fascinating objects that make history come alive. It is a wonderful snap shot back in time of a dynamic period in Stockton history and American history (fig. 14).

One of the most unique and interesting aspects of the museum is its physical location. The collection is housed in the Daguhoy lodge, one of the oldest fraternal organizations in the United States and one of the last remaining links to the historic and powerful Grand Lodge of the Legionarios del Trabajo in America. The lodges played an essential role in the lives of many Filipinos in America and at the Daguhoy Museum the visitor may view the actual setting in which the men lived. Housed in the original, cramped basement of the Daguhoy lodge, which was the actual living space of many of the lodge's Filipino tenants, the museum shows more than any words or pictures the hardship and struggle that the previous generations faced as they made their mark on our United States.

The Daguhoy Filipino Museum is the first Filipino American museum in the Stockton and surrounding areas. It holds a respectable volume of collected memorabilia that displays the many different highlights of the Filipino American experience in Stockton from roughly 1920 to 1970.

Fig. 14—Lorenzo Romano board member of Little Manila Foundation, Dillon Delvo Executive Director of the Little Manila Foundation and GM Antonio Somera also board member of the Little Manila Foundation looking over the many photographs of the early days of Filipino life in America.

Many people do not know that by 1930 California had the largest population of Filipinos in the country with 30, 470. These Filipinos and Filipino Americans made a lasting impression on not only the development of the agricultural giant that we know today as the San Joaquin Valley, but also through their contributions to California, making it one of the largest economical agricultural giants in the United States and the World. Through their farm labor, social activism, and military and civil service these Filipino Americans have truly earned their spot in history as members of America's Greatest Generation.

The Daguhoy Filipino Museum is a private collection of Filipino American artifacts that have been preserved for over 80 years (fig. 15).

Bibliography

Ray A Cabanilia, Floyd E Bongolan. *Blue Book Legionarios Del Trabajo In America 1975* (Ill. Bro. Bart R. Navarro).

Zaide, Gregorio. *Military History of the Philippines* (Uldarico S. Baclagon 1975).

Fig. 15—At the Daguhoy Filipino Museum, L to R setting, GM Antonio Somera, Mayor of Stockton Ed Chavez, Jessica Hernandez, L to R standing, Vince Reyes Urban Legacy director, Fred Mangahas, Dillon Delvo Executive Director Little Manila Foundation, Joaquin Onona, Julian Canete Daguhoy Lodge director, Elena Mangahas Little Manila Foundation.

Part 5
History of Escrima in Stockton

Early History of Escrima in America

The origins of Escrima Filipino Martial Arts in America could be traced back to the late-1500s during the Manila Galleon trade period when Spanish ships brought merchandise across the Pacific using the route from the Philippines to Mexico. Filipinos worked on these ships as sailors and navigators. They were not paid a salary and some say they were worked like slaves. Many of these Filipinos on the Spanish galleons would jump ship in Mexico. Most of these Filipinos had knowledge of Escrima, a Filipino martial art that was taught to them by their family members and by those Filipinos who opposed the Spanish occupation of the Philippines. Some Filipinos would escape to the deepest parts of Mexico, others would run to what is now known as, California, Arizona, New Mexico and Texas. From 1565 to 1815 the records show that many of Filipinos would be forced to cut the wood and build the galleons and be the crewmen and navigators of the Spanish ships that made the journey from the Philippines to Mexico. These early Filipinos were the first Asian immigrants to settle on the Continental United States. Their Spanish masters were so brutal that many Filipinos would try to escape when they landed in Mexico. If the Filipinos were successful, they would build their own villages on stilts and fish for their livelihood in the marshes and bayous in what is called now the state of Louisiana. Filipinos would also settle in the sixteenth century in Acapulco, Mexico. They would easily fit into the Mexican culture and would marry and raise families instilling the Filipino culture in the Mexican way of life. In Louisiana and the Americas, Filipinos can be credited for being the first immigrants to the United States who had initiated the sun-drying process of Louisiana shrimp for export to Canada, Asia and the Americas. Filipinos were also starting their own social clubs in the United States. In 1815 Filipinos also were among the Baratarians who fought with the American smuggler and patriot, the famous Jean Lafitte against the British during the Battle of New Orleans. In 1870 Filipinos had established the first social club, Hispano-Filipino Benevolent Society of New Orleans. Filipinos' early contributions to America were the building blocks for later Filipinos that arrived during the first wave of Filipinos from 1906 to 1934 in modern times.

History of Escrima in Stockton

The history of Escrima in Stockton begins with the first known Filipino to arrive in Stockton, California. It was in 1898 when a clipper ship in San Francisco left behind a Filipino man by the name of Villareal, who joined a Chinese railroad construction gang, bringing him to the central valley of California and eventually to the city of "Mudville" which would later become known as Stockton.

After the Spanish American War in 1898, many Filipinos migrated to the United States for various important reasons, among them education, economics, and adventure—to seek their fame and fortune through the American dream. One of the largest waves of Filipinos coming to America started in 1906 and lasted until 1934. Many of those Filipinos were encouraged to come to the United States by American teachers and misleading advertisements by predatory employers and different shipping companies promising a much better life in America. Unfortunately, the reality of coming to this new land for these fourteen- to twenty-two-year-old Filipinos meant working as "stoop labor" in the agricultural fields of the San Joaquin Valley and in particular Stockton, California (fig. 1).

By 1930 California had the largest population of Filipinos in the country with 30,470. Many of these Filipinos ended up in Stockton, giving the city the nickname "Little Manila." After a hard day's farm work in the fields, these young Filipinos would come into town to socialize, party and to have fun. Sadly enough, coming into town also brought them face to face with racism and prejudice. Despite these dangers, Filipinos came to Stockton to live and play, building a way of life, organizing themselves into small pockets of the population, marry and raise families and to create a Filipino community.

Part 5: History of Escrima in Stockton

Out on necessity and tradition, Filipinos organized themselves into several different fraternal orders. As early as 1920, one of the first Filipino lodges, Caballeros de Dimas-Alang was formed. The second lodge founded in 1920 was the Grand Oriente Filipino, and in 1924 one of the strongest and most powerful of the three lodges was formed, Legionarios del Trabajo.

Many other organizations were formed, such as the Filipino Federation of America, the Filipino Community and others that would get together just as a group of town mates to share each other's company. These lodges and groups would formally meet and be governed by a charter, authorizing duly elected officers to achieve specific objectives by performing ceremonies and rituals. Their objectives were to promote and protect the interests of the Filipino community, while offering wholesome activities for the members, families and friends, including social education and cultural activities.

Fig. 1—Manong Virgil Ibus cutting asparagus at McDonald Island Stockton, California.

As a child I remember attending the lodge's social activities and the willingness of fellow lodge brothers and sisters to help in anyway possible their fellow members. I also remember the many different "uncles" and "aunties" I had because of my father's involvement with the lodge. I would tell my schoolmates that I would have 100 uncles and 100 aunties, not understanding that they were actually my Father's brothers and sisters in the lodge, but this was the Filipino way. We shared a family within a family, which in turn became the foundation of our Filipino heritage here in Stockton and in America. But what I did not know at the time was that many of the men who belonged to these powerful social groups were experts in the arts of Arnis and Escrima. Most of those knowledgeable in Arnis did not teach or share the art with anyone; it was a secret art held in the highest regards. These masters of arnis and escrima would only share their knowledge with a select few, and often their own family members did not know they were arnisadors. All of the 'playing" was done either behind closed doors or deep in the fields and orchards of Stockton to maintain the secrecy of this Filipino martial art. During my research I have found that nearly all of the Filipinos in these fraternal orders played after their meetings behind closed doors.

I can remember as a child that, after the Legionarios' meetings, we were not allowed to go upstairs. I could hear the sounds of sticks clanging and voices of excitement and laughing. I remember even a person guarding the door with a real sword as to not let anyone enter. Someone would approach the door and if they did not give the correct knock on the door or correct phrase or password they would be turned away. I remember one time that after the noise was over, the men would come downstairs talking in Illocano, my father's language. Some were laughing, some arguing, and most of them were carrying long swords strapped to their belt around their waist, and I remember one uncle was carrying a long spear. I thought to myself, what was going on upstairs in the locked room? I had asked the same question to my father who would also be in the locked room and carrying a long sword. "Never mind, we were just playing," he would just say with a smile.

At the outbreak of World War II, Japan attacked Pearl Harbor and the Philippines. When the United States declared war against Japan, many of these same Filipinos volunteered to join the U.S. Armed Forces. So many Filipinos volunteered to join the US Army that orders were issued to activate two regiments: the First Filipino Infantry Regiment to be mobilized in Salinas, California on July 13, 1942, and the Second Filipino Infantry Regiment on November 21, 1942. The First and Second Filipino regiments were at one time one division with the strength of over 12,000 men, consisting of three regiments, plus other special companies. Many of these young Filipinos came from California, especially from the Stockton area, and Hawaii (fig. 2). Out of these 12,000 men a few (less than a thousand) were selected for a special and secret mission. These select few were known as the First Reconnaissance Battalion and were activated on November 20, 1944. The Battalion included the elite 978-Signal Service Company, which was identified with the Allied Intelligence Bureau. These men and officers were called commandos, and their slogan was *Bahala Na*, "Come What May!" They were General MacArthur's secret force, his "eyes and ears," who were dropped behind enemy lines by submarine nearly one year before the American invasion and before any American solider would land on Philippine soil. Their mission was to radio back vital information to General MacArthur, so he can plan his attack and fulfill his promise that "I shall return." These commandos also had a great price on their heads and were considered spies by the Japanese army. The commandos' orders were to avoid

Part 5: History of Escrima in Stockton

detection or identification by the enemy, as this would jeopardize MacArthur's invasion plans for the Philippines. Consequently, countless combat encounters were unrecognized by the US Army since it was necessary to keep the Filipino commandos' mission a secret. The First and Second Filipino Battalions were decorated with the Bronze Star Medal and were awarded many citations for their bravery. Unfortunately, many of these young Filipinos that were in the special Reconnaissance Battalion would only receive the Bronze Star Medal because of the lack of white officers witness the numerous combat encounters and hand-to-hand fighting between the First Reconnaissance Battalion and the enemy. One commando that was assigned to the 978th was Sergeant Leo M. Giron who would become the founder and Grand Master of Bahala Na Filipino Martial Arts Association of Stockton, California.

Fig. 2—Stockton Filipino's allowed to join the United States Military only after a Presidential order.

During the 1950s, only a few World War II veterans and fellow Filipino practitioners would play Arnis Escrima but again only in secret, and most of them would seek out those that practiced the art. Astonishingly enough, most of these arnisadors were members of a local Filipino Lodge people like, Joe Pacpaco, a left-handed arnisador from Santa Catallina, Ilocos Sur, who is a member of the Mabini Lodge in Stockton. Venacio Velle and Clestino S. Somera, who was a member of General Luna #602 Lodge of the Legionarios del Trabajo Stockton, both were excellent *Cabaroan* style players also from Illocos Sur. Victorino Ton who was also from the Legionarios del Trabajo, who was 108 years old when I met him and lived in three different centuries, also played the Carbaroan style. Ton was a good boxer and *cadena de mano* (bare hand, chain of hand) practitioner. Julian Bundoc, from the Barrio Carangay, Bayombang Provice, Pangasianan, was a member of the Filipino community and an expert in the *larga mano* style in addition to being a practitioner of *hilot* (heeling hands). There were icons like Juan Lacaste, who was a member of the Filipino Federation of Stockton and later would be one of Guro Dan Inosanto's Escrima instructors, along with

Escrima legends like Leo M. Giron who was a member of the General Luna Lodge of the Legionarios del Trabajo of Stockton and Angel Cabales, who was a member of the Grand Oriente Filipino Lodge of Stockton. These and other Arnis practitioners would find a way to maintain their skills while maintaining the highest degree of secrecy.

Arnis Escrima would finally be exposed to the general public in the early-1960s, thanks to the early pioneers in Stockton, such as Leo Giron, Angle Cables, Max Sarmiento, Dentoy Revillar, and Dan Inosanto. On discovering that many great masters of Filipino martial arts resided in his own hometown of Stockton, Dan Inosanto preceded to seek them out, record their stories, and present them to the world in his book, *The Filipino Martial Arts*, making Stockton the so-called home of Filipino martial Arts in the United States.

During the 1960s, Angle Cabales taught a few students his *serrada* system above a local restaurant, in downtown Little Manila. These students included Dentoy Revillar and Reno Plaza. Max Sarmiento would drop by on occasion for some lessons. At the same time, Leo Giron was teaching Dentoy Revillar and Max Sarmiento his *larga mano* system at Tracy Defense Depot in Tracy, California. They would train in the back of a warehouse between stacks of wood pallets so no one would see what they were doing, and at times Giron would jump from the stack of pallets to other stacks to simulate different terrain fighting. They would use anything they could find, from aluminum pipes to broom handles and use wide boards as shields.

Dentoy Revillar shared a memorable story with me. At one time when he and Giron were sparring, he thought he had Giron in his angle to catch him with a number three strike, to Giron's left hip. Revillar counter blocked and quickly delivered the number three strike and Giron, using the *estilo elastico* technique, ducked completely under Revillar's strike. Revillar could not believe it and was consequently caught himself in the midsection by Giron's own counter strike.

It was also said that Giron could not be hit; you could not get close enough to him; you would get hit first from Giron's weapon. Giron also has the best body evade angle: The weapon would also get so close to him, and you can see him watch the weapon glide right by his body without getting hit. His striking angles were so direct and clean that he always had his weapon on me.

It wouldn't be until the mid-1960s that Stockton, or even America, would be publicly exposed to the Filipino martial arts. Lynn Sarmiento (Max Sarmiento's wife) and Dentoy Revillar helped Angel Cabales open his first commercial Escrima school in America. This would open the door for many other masters of the art to become known and open schools of their own. But according to my research, Cabales was not the first choice to head the new enterprise that would introduce to the public the teaching of Filipino martial arts. It was the uncle of Max Sarmiento who was going to lead and teach the art of Arnis Escrima at the academy. But due to family obligations Max Sarmiento's uncle had to return to the Philippines. However, Sarmiento would approach Angle Cabales and request Cabales to take over the academy. Lynn Sarmiento would be the force behind the organization of his newly formed alliance.

Leo Giron had already made the acquaintance of Cabales through the many social events that were held by the different Filipino lodges in Stockton. One day, Cabales, Revillar, and Sarmiento invited Giron to come and visit the Cabales academy located next to Gong Lee's restaurant. Giron would on occasion drop in and play Arnis Escrima and help teach the students. Cabales, Giron, Revillar and Sarmiento had planned of forming the biggest Filipino martial arts academy in the United States. Cabales would teach *serrada*, Giron would teach *larga mano*, Sarmiento would teach *cadena de mano*, and Revillar would assist all three. However, after the killing of eight student nurses, two of them Filipina, in 1966, Giron decided to open his own club in Tracy, California.

Since Giron still wanted to be a part of the enterprise and associated with Cabales, Sarmiento and Reviler, he approached Cabales to request support to continue his association with the group. Cabales asked Giron how many students he had in Tracy. Giron answered that he had six, and Cabales replied that six were not enough for him to travel and teach in Tracy. Giron answered that he didn't want Cabales to teach his students, but rather he merely wanted to remain part of Cabales's Escrima association. Thereafter, Cabales and Giron parted ways, and Giron continued to teach at his club in Tracy and Cabales in Stockton. Giron would still, on occasion visit Angel Cabales to help and to demonstrate his style of *larga mano* & *cabaroan*. Giron did not teach anyone else from the Stockton academy on a regular basis, but only would drop in from time to time to visit. Many people have claimed to train with Giron in his *larga mano* system from the Stockton academy at Gong Lee, which is true but only in a *minimal* amount of classroom training. Only those graduates who are listed on the Bahala Na Martial Arts website have completed the comprehensive system of training that is required by the Bahala Na Martial Arts Association Constitution and By-Laws in the Giron system.

In 1973 Giron relocated his residence and Arnis Escrima Club to South Stockton. It was not until the groundbreaking research of Dan Inosanto that the world of Filipino martial arts in Stockton was exposed through his articles and book (fig. 3). The masters from Stockton featured in that book included Leo M. Giron of the *cabaroan* and *cadaanan larga mano* styles, a member of the Legionarios del Trabajo; Angel Cabales of the *serrada* style; Regino Ellustrisimo of the Bohol and Ellustrisimo styles; Juanito LaCaste of the *espada y daga* style and member of the Filipino Federation; Dentoy Revillar of the *serrada, larga mano* and *decuerdas* styles; Max Sarmiento of the *cadena de mano* and *daga* styles; and Gilbert Tenio of the *decuerdas* style and a member of the Legionarios del Trabajo. Without question, Stockton was the birthplace of Filipino martial arts in the United States.

Fig. 3—GME Giron and Guro Dan Inosanto "playing" Escrima in the backyard of Giron, Stockton, California.

In the late-1970s and early-1980s, history would repeat itself. Max Sarmiento, Dentoy Revillar, Leo Giron and Dan Inosanto would attempt to unite all Arnis and Escrima academies in California into the biggest organization of Filipino martial arts in America. The name West Coast Escrima Society would be that attempt at unification. Unfortunately, the lack of ability to communicate and travel amongst the members would make it impossible to fulfill this dream. Although the west Coast Escrima Society continued on for several years, many of the members would attempt to serve and promote the Filipino arts in their own fashion. They sponsored several tournaments, conducted workshops and seminars of various systems and styles, and encouraged other groups to continue on a smaller scale of Filipino art unification and promotion. Even today, nearly thirty five years later, subgroups of the West Coast Escrima Society are still active but have returned to their own groups and in nearly all cases have renamed their organizations only to keep the memories of our forefathers alive by teaching, learning, sharing and spreading the Filipino arts.

During the late 1980s and early 1990s, there was another attempt to unite the Arnis and Escrima groups into one organization, this time on a smaller scale and just focusing on the Stockton groups (fig. 4). It would once again be Leo M. Giron, Dentoy Revillar, and John Eliab who united the three major systems in Stockton to form the Escrima Coalition. In doing so, other Stockton Arnis groups came to join and support the promotion of the Filipino arts. In the next ten years, the Stockton-based Arnis Escrima practitioners conducted tournaments and supported local nonprofit groups through their fund raising efforts (fig 5).

Fig. 4—GME Leo M. Giron and Guro Dentoy Revillar after an Escrima Coalition tournament. Dentoy would always host a BBQ for members and volunteers of the Coalition tournament at his home with his famous BBQ rib's. Dentoy was an early student and graduate of GME Giron.

Fig. 5—Guro Dentoy Revillar giving final instructions and rules before a Coalition tournament held in Stockton, California.

Fig. 6—Guests of honor Mr. & Mrs. Sebastian Inosanto after a Bahala Na Graduation ceremony. Mrs. Inosanto was a practicing member of Bahala Na Martial Arts Association.

Even with the Escrima Coalitions retirement in the year 2000, many of the Stockton groups still keep in contact and promoted the art together.

Today, over 100 years after the first known Filipino to arrive in Stockton, California, this little farming town has gained international fame for being the root of Filipino martial arts in America. Our forefathers planted the seeds, and even today, Stockton remains a stronghold of knowledge and growth in Arnis Escrima as it maintains the dreams of those early pioneers who took the chance of exposing the secret fighting arts of the Philippines (fig. 6). Bahala Na!

Bibliography

Cordova, Fred. *Forgotten Asian Americans* (Dubuque: Kendall/Hunt, 1983).

Part 6
Last of the Bladed Warriors

Grand Master Emeritus Leo Giron was born in Bayambang, in the province of Pangasinan, Phillipines. He was a World War II veteran and was awarded the Bronze Star medal amongst many other citations. As the head advisor and also the founder of Bahala Na Martial Arts Association, he was world renown as the Father of Larga Mano in America. Until the last day of his life, Grand Master Giron was active and teaching along with Grand Master Antonio E. Somera at the home base school in Stockton, California. His knowledge of jungle warfare was an invaluable asset to those that trained with him. His appearance was that of a humble man with the character of a distinguish college professor. Grandmaster Giron talked, looked and carried himself with an uncommon class and style. There was something distinctive about him. Maybe it was something you only get when you fight against men whom would like to take your life away.

Q: When were you inducted into the Army?
A: I was inducted on October 9, 1942 this was in Los Angeles California because prier to this I was farming in Imperial Valley California. I was first stationed at Camp San Luis Obispo, and then in the winter of the same year I was transferred to Fort Ord.

Q: How were you selected to be in the 978th signal service company?

A: Well, everyone was brought into a big room, it was the recreation room on base. This is where we were given an aptitude test. Many did not pass and they were sent back to their regiments. Others made it and were given additional education on Morse code. The Army was looking for specific types of men. They were looking for men with schooling and how well they could communicate including speaking English. I was one of the few that made it.

Q: What was your training experience like in the Army?

A: During boot camp we also went to school. We were learning communications like Morse code, wig-wag (flag signals), cyma four, cryptography and paraphrasing. I was trained to communicate. At the time I did not know what the Army was planning for me to do. We were never told why we were training; you just did what the Army told you to do.

Q: What type of self-defense training did you receive from the Army?

A: We learned all the basic training needed for soldiering. Nothing special just how to shoot a carbine, how to use a .45 and some basic hand-to-hand combat. I was fortunate to learn escrima as a child and later after coming to America with one of my most influential teachers Flaviano Vergara. Flaviano is the man that taught me the most about escrima and how to defend myself. In fact I met Flaviano a second time in Fort Ord during which time we would play on weekdays after dinner on the weekends while everyone went into town. Flaviano and I would do nothing but drill and drill using estilo de fondo and larga mano. Sometimes a soldier would come by and ask what were we doing? Some would tell us that they would never come close to a Samurai sword. They claimed they would give the Samurai a load of their M-1.

Q: How were your first experiences with the art of Escrima?
A: It was very interesting because as kids every time we—my friends and me—heard the 'click, click, click' of knives, we would be playing under the mango trees and the trail would be guarded. I sneaked away to watch. Later, we paid so many bundles of straw and rice for our lesson. My family didn't know. I was carrying a bundle or rice when my father asked me about it and I told him I was going to take it to my uncle; we were going to make cakes! In one of my first training session my instructor told me: "take your bolo and let's do some training. Don't worry about hurting me because I've been fighting for a long time. Cut me anytime you can. If you touch me you'll get a month's pay." That was the way you learned in those days. I learnt a lot about how to use the environment for survival purposes. This is a very important aspect, especially when you're fighting in the jungle. You need to know how to maximize every tree, every bush, the smallest help may be what you need to save your life.

Q: Would you please tell us about all your instructors and the system they taught you?
A: I had five teachers and I will give them to you in order and what style they passed onto me.

1. Benito Junio from the barrio of Inerangan town of Bayombang province of Pangasinan, Luzon Philippines. In 1920 I started my education in arnis escrima. Benito Junio was famous for his larga mano (long hand-stick) and fondo fuerte (fighting in a solid position) styles.

2. Fructuso Junio from the barrio of Telbang town of Bayombang provice of Pangasinan, Luzon Philippines. From 1921-1926 I continued my training with Fructuso uncle to Bentio. Fructuso Junio was well-known for his Macabebe or two-stick fighting. Fructuso was the first to share with Giron the importance of distinguishing between the old (cada-anan) and new (cabaroan) styles of Luzon.

3. Flavian Vergara from Santa Curz in Llocos Sur Luzon, Philippines. Vergara was the top student of Dalmacio Bergonia who defeated the great champion Santiago Toledo. Vergara and I started our training in the prune orchards of Meridian, Calif., from 1929-1932. Vergara and Giron would meet again directly after the outbreak of World War II. Our lives would cross for the last time in October 1942 when I was shipped out to Fort Ord, Calif. Every spare minute Vergara and I would train until I was shipped out

in January, 1943. Vergara was a master in the Bergonia style and very proficient in the estilo elastico (rubber band style). I always thought that Vergara had superhuman abilities. Vergara influenced me a lot and his understanding of the relationships between the cada-anan (old) and cabaroan (new) styles of arnis escrima.

4. Beningo Ramos from Kongkong Bayongbang. During World War II Ramos was a sergeant in the Filipino army assigned to me. Pryor to the outbreak of World War II Ramos was an improbable arnis escrima teacher and was respected as one of the best estilo matador (killer-style) teachers in Luzon. Ramos was an expert in larga mano, miscla contras, tero pisada, tero grave and elastico styles. Ramos was so confident of his skills that he and I would play with live bolos. Ramos bet me that if I could hit him he would give me one month's pay. I never collected a cent from Ramos.

5. Julian Bundoc from the barrio of Carangay town of Bayombang province of Pangasianan, Luzon Philippines. Julian was cousin to Benito Junio. Julian Bundoc and I would play more of the combative larga mano and work on conditioning the body. Julian Bundoc was also a master of hilot or massage. We trained in Stockton from 1956-1961.

One of my teachers named Flaviano Vergara had the most influence on me and helped me greatly in developing my system.

Q: How many systems or methods comprise your own personal method and what are their characteristics?

A: I'm well-known around the world for my larga mano style of escrima. But this is just a small piece of the entire Giron arnis escrima system. The Giron system has 20 styles and techniques that are just as effective and just as complete.

Q: When did you decided to go overseas?

A: On December 10, 1943 two of us were shipped to New Guinea but this was a mistake by the Army we were suppose to go to Australia. So on January 10, 1944

I was sent to Australia to a place called Camp X. It was close to the little town of Beau Desert about 60 miles from the seaport of Brisbane in Queens land. It was there that I furthered my training in Morse code, cryptography, visual communications, etc. I also embarked on my final training in jungle warfare in a place called Canungra.

Thirteen weeks of hard training contributed to my ability in climbing the high mountains of the Philippines and surviving in the jungles. At one time for a weeks period we were given only 3 days of sea rations and the

Part 6: Last of the Bladed Warriors

other 4 days we were to survive on our own. At this point I was Staff Sergeant.

Q: Did you ever meet General Douglas MacArthur?
A: Yes, several times but on August 10, 1944 I was ordered to a briefing at the General's Headquarters. General MacArthur crossed his arms and said to us, "Boys, I selected you to do a job that a general can't do. You have the training to do a job that no one else can do. You are going home to our country, the Philippines—yours and my homeland. You'll serve as my eyes, my ears, and my fingers, and you'll keep me informed of what the enemy is doing. You will tell me how to win the war by furnishing me with this information, which I could not obtain in any other way. Good luck, and there will be shining bars waiting for you in Manila."

Q: How did you land in the Philippines?
A: August 12, 1944, we boarded one of the smallest submarines in the United States Navy armada. The US Sting Ray, we were loaded and armed with carbines, sub machine guns, side arms, bolo knives, trench knives, brass knuckles ammunition and a few other special packages. While on our way to the Philippines we slept on our own cargo boxes. Myself and one other

soldier slept under the torpedo racks. There was one time when we were fired upon and had to out maneuver several torpedoes at full speed. This occurred near the Halmahera Island on the Celebes Sea. One other time when we were attacked was in Caonayan Bay just before disembarking the submarine. The attack was in the submarine when a plane had dropped depth charges on us. They came close enough to rattle the sub and burst some pipes but luckily this was the extent of the damage. We landed on the beach on August 28, 1944.

Q: What was the most memorable encounter you had with the enemy?

A: Well it is hard to try and choose one particular encounter because they were all very horrifying. One bonsai attack comes to mind, in early June 1945 on a rainy day a large size of enemy charged against our position. We would form in wedge or triangle formation, two on the side and one as point man, I was point man. Just like any Bonsai charge the enemy was always noisy. Yelling and shouting, they are not afraid to die. The Filipino guerrillas on the other hand chew their tobacco, grit their teeth and wing their bolos, chop here, jab there long bolos, short daggers, pointed bamboo, pulverized chili peppers with sand deposited in bamboo tubes to spray so the enemy cannot see. By now by adrenaline must have gone up, one bayonet and samurai sword came simultaneously. The samurai sword was in front of me while the bayonet was little to the left. With my left hand I parried the bayonet, I blocked the sword coming down on me, the bayonet man went by and his body came in line with my bolo when I came down to cut his left

Part 6: Last of the Bladed Warriors

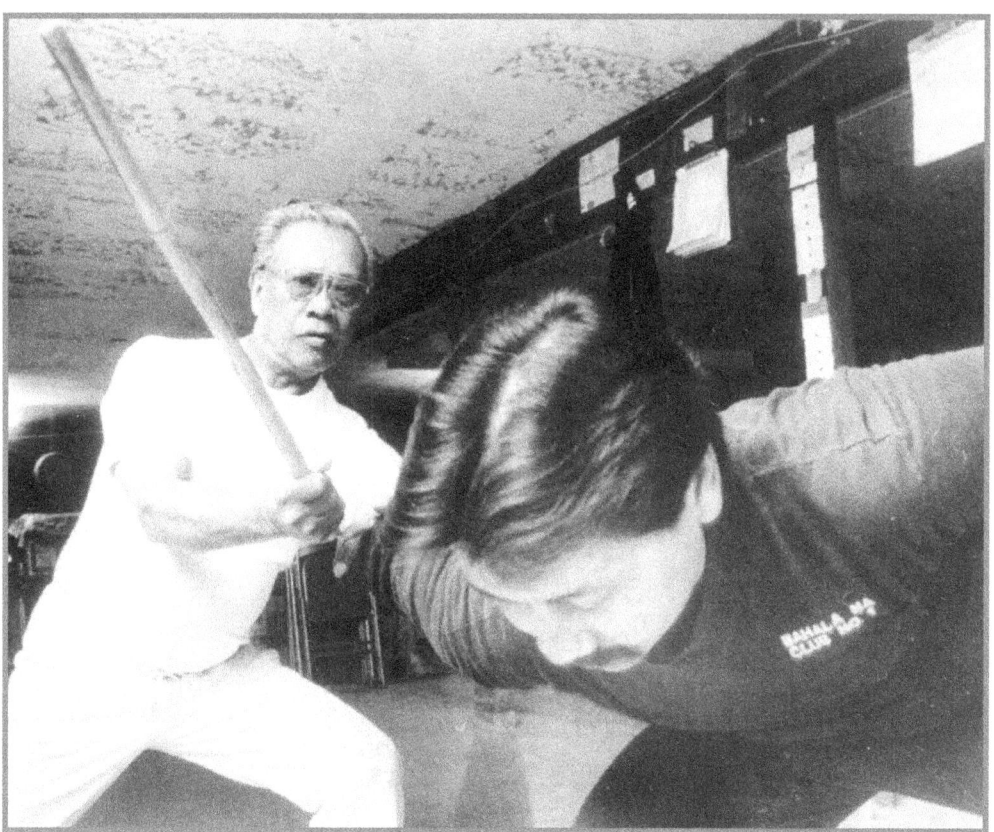

hip. The samurai was coming back with a backhand blow. I met his tricep with the bolo chopping it to the ground. After the encounter I wiped my face with my left hand to clear my eyes from the rain and found bloodstains on my face. The boys told me, blood sir I felt the twitch on the meaty part of my left palm when I parried the bayonet. I didn't know I was cut. There were many more encounters. But our job was not to be detected by the enemy; our mission was to send back vital information of the enemy to head quarters.

Q: When did you start teaching the art of arnis escrima?

A: In October 1968 I decided to open a club in Tracy, California, where I was residing at the time. I was motivated after I heard on the news that a man in Chicago killed eight nursing students and some of the nurses were Filipinas.

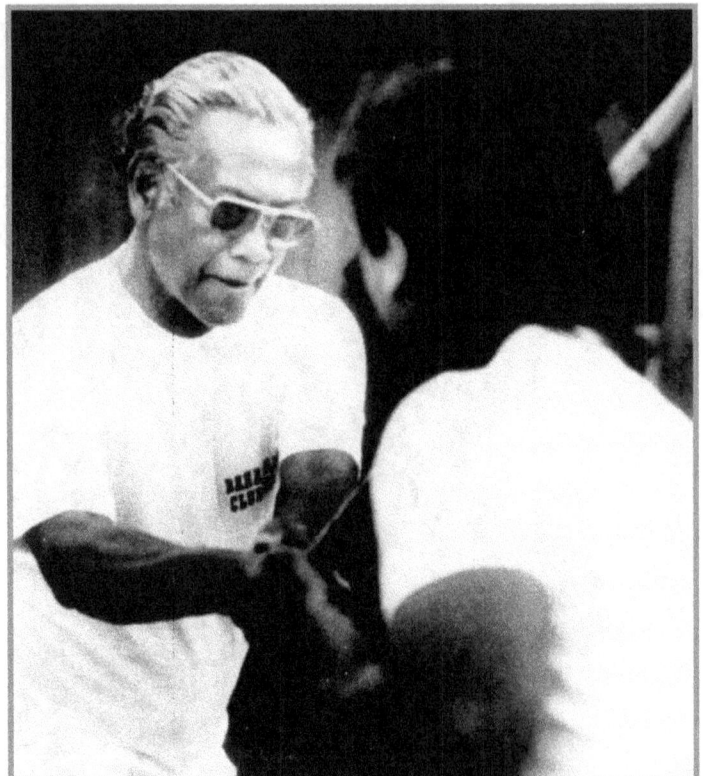

Q: Why did you name your Martial Art Association "Bahala Na"?

A: It was the slogan of my outfit during World War II. I am proud of the men I fought with during World War II and in the spirit of my comrades; I hold the memories of all of those I fought with in very high regard and close to my heart. I also can associate the combative spirit we had during the time of World War II and because of this I feel I have the right to use the slogan of "Bahala Na" by the way it means "come what may."

Q: What makes a good student?

A: A person with good passive resistance. You must have patience and not be too eager to win and be the champion. What he should be interested in is to learn how to defend himself and his family against aggression and the end result will be that you will survive this makes you victorious. You do not need to say I am going to win and defeat my opponent the attitude is that I am going to survive and not get hurt that's what will count, the other man will eventually fall into a loophole were he will fall by himself and eventually he will defeat himself.

Q: Do you feel that your experience during World War II in the jungles of the Philippines help you to become a better teacher.

A: I know the respect of the bolo knife. Wartime is different. There is no regard for life. It's different teaching; you must have structure and good communications with your students. I like to teach more about the application and fundamentals. Its not about how hard you hit or who is faster, its about sharing the art of our forefathers, because if you analyze it we are only the caretakers of the art for future generations.

Q: Why do you still teach escrima?

A: Well first it's a hobby. I have the chance to stretch my legs, work my arms and exercise my body. I feel it is a gift to be able to learn a combative art like escrima and being that it falls in the field of sports it is good to have and know something that not to many people know. I feel proud that I have something to share with the children my friends and those that want to learn an art that is a little different than other martial arts. I feel that the Filipino art is a superior art in comparison to other arts, so I stand firm in saying that I am proud that I have learned and still know the art of escrima.

Q: In the past there has been many masters that have fought in death matches. Have you ever fought in any death matches?

A: No, I have never fought in a death match. From what I understand, in order to participate in a death match you will need to have a referee and a second or back up person in your corner, something similar to a boxing match. The only type of death match I had it was during World War II. This is were I fought in the jungles for over a year, not knowing if we would survive. Our weapons of choice were the bolo knife or Talonason, a long knife—it's overall length was 36 inches long. No referee, no rules. The only rule was to survive.

Q: What's your advice to the martial art practitioners?

A: It seems to be an unstoppable growing mentality of the 'fighting' in the martial arts community. I fought for my life in a real war, and that's not pleasant. Practitioners should focus on the general benefits of martial arts from self-defense to a way of life instead of trying to be a 'deadly fighting machine.' We should strive to be better human being. That's the final goal of any martial art, to preserve life, not to destroy it.

Part 7
Twenty Styles of Grand Master Leo M. Giron

From the front of the famous "Masters Fan" of Grand Master Emeritus Leo M. Giron system of arnis Escrima. The following are the names and a brief overview of each of the 20 styles (estilo) that encompass the Giron method of Escrima:

Estilo de Fondo—This is a style of planting yourself firmly on the ground. During combat you do not want to move your feet about, as this may cause you to lose your footing and balance. This style counters off the 12 angles of attack using a stick in length of 24 inches, which simulates the bolo. There are approximately 175 counter movements in this style.

Estilo de Abanico—This is a fanning style encompassing the use of the side of the weapon (stick or blade) to block oncoming attacks. Counterstriking is included with the emphasis on the tip of your weapon to get the maximum amount of power in short and powerful striking ranges.

Estilo de Abierta—This style refers to an open body style of fighting. The most advanced students use this style to calculate the distance between themselves and their opponent. The student will calculate the opponent's strikes and will open his body position and counterstrike within the same motion, leaving the opponent with little or no counter.

GME Giron and GM Somera with the 20 styles of the "Masters Fan."

Estilo de Salon—This is a dance-like style. This style uses fast and solid footwork that also involves the use of stick work.

Estilo Sonkete—This is the style of poking and thrusting. As your opponent attacks you can use the components of parrying, blocking, evading, and deflection while applying the counterthrust or poke into the opponent's guard.

Estilo Retirada—This is a style of retreating used to draw your opponent in or to create an opening in the opponent's defense. Once this has taken place you can use counterstriking to render your opponent helpless. Retreating footwork, evading, and counterstriking is the key.

Estilo Elastico—An elastic-like or rubber band style. It makes use of one's stretching ability to reach a given target. This style is a necessity that is woven into the larga mano (long hand) style. Many feel that the person who plays estilo elastico possesses superhuman ability and is difficult to defeat.

Fondo Fuerte—The escrimador's last stand. You must plant yourself effectively into a reliable spot where you can revolve to meet an opponent's attacks without losing ground.

Contra Compas—These Spanish words mean against time. In terms of Giron arnis escrima this is a style of striking with off-beat timing or broken rhythm.

Estilo Redonda—This style is comprised of round or circular weapon movements which are effective when surrounded by multiple opponents, or when faced with a seasoned practitioner who needs to be kept at bay. While playing this style you must maintain a continuous circular motion with your weapon. A horizontal circle to the ankle and then a horizontal circle to the head is an example. Estilo redonda can also be used in striking along a vertical circle, both forward and reverse. This style is mainly used for offensive, continuous striking. If your weapon is hit or blocked, you can quickly reverse the circle to maintain your aggressive circular striking style.

Combate Adentro—This style is used to ward off opponents using paired weapons, such as the sword and dagger. With this style, you defend yourself inside the opponent's circle using solid footwork and slicing counterstrikes.

Estilo Macabebe—Macabebe is the name of a town in the province of Pampanga, Philippines. These fierce warriors are famous for the use of two weapons or two sticks. This style is characterized by the interweaving motions of the weapons and is also known as sinawali

Tero Pisada—This style incorporates the use of double or two-handed striking and blocking. The blocking is so intense that it will paralyze the opponent's hands and will create an opening for your two-handed counterstrike.

Media Media—The term media media implies half of half. In terms of fighting, the concept refers to fighting at half-range and striking on half-timing.

Cadena de Mano—This is a hand-to-hand combat method, which uses parrying, grabbing, twisting, locking, and choking in succession. In other words, you chain the hand movements together from close quarters.

Escapo—This style stresses evasion and methods of warding off the opponents.

Estilo Bolante—This style is named after a person named Braulio Bolante from Dagupan, Pagasinan, Philippines. This style uses vertical striking patterns and is an excellent method of fighting in doorways and narrow passages.

Tero Grave—This style implies the use of serious or deadly strikes to critical areas of the body.

Miscla (Mezcla) Contras—This style favors defending against multiple opponents and multiple attacks. It stresses placing oneself in the proper place and position in relation to the opponent.

Larga mano—This style maintains long-distance fighting without jeopardizing safety. The counter concept is that of attacking the closest target of your opponent and to terminate the contest with the first counterstrike.

1
Estilo de Fondo

Outside block #1

1 McCune prepares to deliver a number 1 strike to Somera's left collarbone.

2 Somera steps to 11 o'clock with his left foot and counter strikes to McCune's right outside wrist.

3 Somera chambers his weapon to his right side and "C" checks McCune's weapon arm.

4 Somera counter strikes McCune's right outside forearm.

Inside block #1

McCune prepares to deliver a number 1 strike to Somera's left collarbone

Somera steps to 1 o'clock with his right foot and counter strikes McCune's weapon arm

Somera adjust his left foot to 6 o'clock, Somera chambers his weapon to the 4 heavy striking position, with his left hand Somera grabs McCune's weapon wrist

Part 7: Twenty Styles of Grand Master Leo M. Giron

Somera counter strikes McCune's right mid section.

Somera continues his counter striking with a number 11 to McCune's right femoral artery.

Somera finishes his counter strike to McCune with a number 2 strike to McCune's collarbone.

Giron Escrima

Sweep block LFL #2

McCune prepares to deliver a number 2 strike to Somera's right collarbone

Somera steps to 11 o'clock with his left foot and applies an outside sweep block and applies a "C" check with his left hand to McCune's right forearm.

Somera counter strikes McCune's right outside forearm.

Part 7: Twenty Styles of Grand Master Leo M. Giron

4

Somera follows up with a number 9 strike to McCune's right outside forearm.

5

Somera chambers his weapon to his right side and "C" checks McCune's weapon arm.

Giron Escrima

Fan to Mid section #2

McCune prepares to deliver a number 2 strike to Somera's right collarbone

Somera steps to 1 o'clock with his right foot, Somera ducks and counter strikes McCune's inside weapon arm with the tip of his weapon.

Somera chambers his weapon to his right side and "C" checks McCune's weapon arm.

Part 7: Twenty Styles of Grand Master Leo M. Giron

Somera follows up with a number 4 strike to McCune's mid section.

Somera continues his counter striking with a number 11 to McCune's right femoral artery.

Somera finishes his counter strike to McCune with a number 2 strike to McCune's right side collarbone.

Down beat #3

McCune prepares to deliver a number 3 strike to Somera's left hip.

Somera counter blocks McCune's strike with a deflection using the flat side of his bolo knife, deflecting down and out to Somera's right side.

Somera steps to 1 o'clock with his right foot, Somera checks McCune with this left hand and counter strikes McCune's outside forearm using the tip of his weapon.

Part 7: Twenty Styles of Grand Master Leo M. Giron

4

Somera maintains his left hand check and chambers his weapon to his right side.

5

Somera counter strikes McCune's right outside forearm with the tip of his blade.

Left hand check #3

McCune prepares to deliver a number 3 strike to Somera's left hip.

Somera steps to 11 o'clock with his left foot and checks McCune with a "C" check using his left hand.

Somera will parry McCune's weapon hand down and to Somera's right side and prepares to slice McCune's right inside forearm.

Part 7: Twenty Styles of Grand Master Leo M. Giron

4

Somera follows through and counter strikes McCune's right outside forearm using the tip of his weapon.

5

Somera steps to 1 o'clock with his right foot, Somera checks McCune with this left hand and prepares to counter strikes McCune.

6

Somera counter strikes McCune's right outside forearm with the tip of his blade.

X block #4

McCune prepares to deliver a number 4 strike to Somera's right hip.

Somera steps to 1 o'clock with his right foot, Somera checks McCune with this left hand and counter block McCune's using the flat side of Somera's weapon.

Somera will parry McCune's weapon hand down to Somera's left side and prepares to counter strike McCune left side.

Part 7: Twenty Styles of Grand Master Leo M. Giron

Somera continues his counter striking with a number 11 to McCune's right femoral artery.

Somera finishes his counter strike to McCune with a number 2 strike to McCune's right side collarbone.

Giron Escrima

Down beat back of bolo #4

McCune prepares to deliver a number 4 strike to Somera's right hip.

Somera steps to 1 o'clock with his right foot, Somera checks McCune with this left hand and counter block McCune's using the back side of Somera's weapon.

Somera parry's down and out and continues his counter striking with a number 11 to McCune's mid section.

Somera finishes his counter strike to McCune with a number 2 strike to McCune's right side collarbone.

Left hand check to #5

McCune prepares to deliver a number 5 strike to Somera's mid section.

Somera steps to 11 o'clock with his left foot and applies a outside sweep block and applies a "C" check with his left hand to McCune's right forearm.

Somera follows through and counter strikes McCune's right outside forearm using the tip of his weapon.

Cross to Bartical #5

1
McCune prepares to deliver a number 5 strike to Somera's mid section.

2
Somera steps to 1 o'clock with his right foot, Somera checks McCune with this left hand and counter blocks McCune's bolo pointing down and using the flat side of Somera's weapon.

3
Somera maintains his left hand grip and counter strikes McCune inside right weapon forearm.

4
Somera continues his counter striking with a number 11 to McCune's right femoral artery.

2
Estilo de Abanico

Giron Escrima

Outside block to abanico hit #1

McCune prepares to deliver a number 1 strike to Somera's left collarbone.

Somera steps to 9 o'clock with his left foot and applies a outside block using the flat side of his blade

Somera abanico flip hits to McCune's outside forearm.

Part 7: Twenty Styles of Grand Master Leo M. Giron

4
Somera steps to 1 o'clock with his right foot; Somera checks McCune with this left hand and chambers his weapon to his right side.

5
Somera follows through and counter strikes McCune's right outside forearm using the tip of his weapon.

Giron Escrima

Inside left hand check #1

McCune prepares to deliver a number 1 strike to Somera's left collarbone.

Somera abanico flip hits to McCune's outside shoulder and "C" check McCune's inside wrist.

Somera abanico flip hits to McCune's left temple and maintains his left-handed grip on McCune.

Part 7: Twenty Styles of Grand Master Leo M. Giron

Somera prepares to chop McCune's forearm.

Somera will finish by a chop down on McCune's forearm.

Giron Escrima

Left hand downward check to abanico hits #2

1 McCune prepares to deliver a number 2 strike to Somera's right collarbone.

2 Somera steps to 1 o'clock with his right foot, Somera checks McCune with this left hand and counter strikes McCune's right shoulder.

3 Somera will parry McCune's weapon down and out then abanico flip hit to McCune's left temple and maintains his left-handed grip on McCune.

4 Somera prepares to chop McCune's forearm.

Part 7: Twenty Styles of Grand Master Leo M. Giron

5

Somera chops McCune's forearm.

6

Somera clears his weapon and chamber to his left side.

7

Somera follows through and counter strikes McCune's right side using the tip of his weapon.

Fan to mid section #2

McCune prepares to deliver a number 2 strike to Somera's right collarbone.

Somera steps to 1 o'clock with his right foot ducks under the strike and counter blocks McCune's strike using the flat side of his blade.

Somera abanico flip hits to McCune's left temple and "C" checks McCune's inside weapon wrist.

Part 7: Twenty Styles of Grand Master Leo M. Giron

4 Somera abanico and chops down on McCune's forearm.

5 Somera clears his weapon and chambers to his left side.

6 Somera maintains his left hand grip and will finish his counter strike to McCune mid section.

Bending mid section to abanico hits #3

McCune prepares to deliver a number 3 strike to Somera's left hip.

Somera will bend at his mid section, outside left hand parry's to McCune's weapon hand and will counter strike with an abanico inside hit using the tip of Somera's weapon.

Somera abanico flip hits to McCune's outside weapon hand.

Part 7: Twenty Styles of Grand Master Leo M. Giron

4

Somera steps to 1 o'clock with his right foot, "C" checks McCune's weapon hand and prepares to counter strike McCune.

5

Somera finish his counter strikes to McCune's right outside forearm using the tip of his blade.

Down beat hard to abanico hits #3

McCune prepares to deliver a number 3 strike to Somera's left hip.

Somera will bend at his mid section and deflect down with his weapon using the flat side of the blade to McCune's weapon.

Somera will step to 1 o'clock with his right foot and "C" check with his left hand to McCune's weapon hand striking McCune's weapon hand with an abanico hit.

Part 7: Twenty Styles of Grand Master Leo M. Giron

Somera maintains his left hand grip and chambers his weapon to his left side.

Somera finishes his counter strikes to McCune's right outside forearm using the tip of his blade.

Giron Escrima

Bending mid section abanico hits #4

1. McCune prepares to deliver a number 4 strike to Somera's right hip.

2. Somera will bend at his mid section and will direct abanico hit to McCune's outside weapon hand, checking McCune with his left hand.

3. Somera will follow up with an abanico hit to the inside of McCune's inside wrist and will parry McCune's weapon hand down.

4. Somera clears McCune's weapon hand down and out and step's to 1 o'clock with his right foot and will finish with a strike to McCune's right collarbone.

Left hand downward check to abanico temple hits #4

1 McCune prepares to deliver a number 4 strike to Somera's right hip.

2 Somera will bend at his mid section and will direct abanico hit to McCune's left temple, checking McCune with his left hand.

3 Somera will follow up with an abanico hit to McCune's right temple and will parry McCune's weapon hand down.

4 Somera will finish with an abanico chop to McCune's inside arm.

Outside left hand check to abanico hits #5

McCune prepares to deliver a number 5 strike to Somera's mid section.

Somera steps to 11 o'clock with his left foot, parries McCune's to the inside and abanico hit to McCune's inside forearm.

Somera will follow up with an outside abanico hit to McCune's outside forearm.

Part 7: Twenty Styles of Grand Master Leo M. Giron

4

Somera "C" checks McCune's weapon hand and chambers his weapon to his right side.

5

Somera follows through and counter strikes McCune's right side using the tip of his weapon.

Giron Escrima

Inside left hand check to abanico hits #5

1. McCune prepares to deliver a number 5 strike to Somera's mid section.

2. Somera steps to 12 o'clock left hand checks McCune's weapon using the flat side of his palm and abanico strike to McCune's inside forearm.

3. Somera follows up with an abanico strike to McCune's outside forearm.

4. Somera will finish with an abainco strike to McCune's left temple and will grab McCune's weapon wrist.

3
Estilo de Abierta

Giron Escrima

#1 Outside follow

McCune prepares to deliver a number 1 strike to Somera's left collarbone. Somera is in a ready position.

Somera rotates his right shoulder and points his right foot towards 3 o'clock allowing McCune's strike to pass closely by Somera's shoulder, Somera counter strikes to McCune's outside weapon wrist.

Somera steps to 1 o'clock with his right foot and "C" checks McCune's weapon forearm with his left hand, Somera chambers his weapon to his right side.

Somera counter strikes McCune's weapon forearm.

#2 Inside follow

McCune prepares to deliver a number 2 strike to Somera's right collarbone. Somera is in a ready position.

Somera rotates his left shoulder and points his left foot towards 9 o'clock allowing McCune's strike to pass closely by Somera's shoulder, Somera counter strikes to McCune's inside weapon wrist.

Somera steps to 1 o'clock with his right foot, grabs McCune's weapon inside wrist and counter strikes McCune's right collarbone.

#3 Outside follow

1
McCune prepares to deliver a number 11 strike to Somera's left hip. Somera is in a ready position.

2
Somera rotates his right knee and points his right foot towards 3 o'clock allowing McCune's strike to pass closely by Somera's knee, Somera counter strikes to McCune's outside weapon wrist.

3
Somera steps to 1 o'clock with his right foot and "C" checks McCune's weapon forearm with his left hand, Somera chambers his weapon to right side.

4
Somera counter strikes McCune's weapon forearm.

Part 7: Twenty Styles of Grand Master Leo M. Giron

#4 Inside follow

1 McCune prepares to deliver a number 9 strike to Somera's right hip. Somera is in a ready position.

2 Somera rotates his left knee and points his left foot towards 9 o'clock allowing McCune's strike to pass closely by Somera's knee, Somera counter strikes to McCune's inside weapon wrist.

3 Somera steps to 1 o'clock with his right foot, grabs McCune's weapon inside wrist and counter strikes McCune's right collarbone.

Giron Escrima

#5 Inside follow

McCune prepares to deliver a number 5 strike to Somera's mid section. Somera is in a ready position.

Somera evades McCune's strike and steps back with his left foot to 6 o'clock, Somera strikes to the inside of McCune's inside forearm.

Somera steps to 1 o'clock with his right foot, grabs McCune's weapon inside wrist and counter strikes McCune's right collarbone.

4
Estilo de Salon

Giron Escrima

The goal is footwork and the ability to dance and move to evade and encounter the opponent.

Part 7: Twenty Styles of Grand Master Leo M. Giron

5
Estilo Sonkete

Part 7: Twenty Styles of Grand Master Leo M. Giron

Outside block to #6

1 McCune prepares to deliver a number 1 strike to Somera's left collarbone. Somera is in a ready position.

2 Somera steps forward to 11 o'clock with his left foot, parry's McCune's weapon hand to the inside and counter block McCune's weapon using an asparagus knife.

3 Somera leans forward and pokes McCune's right collarbone and parrying McCune's weapon hand to the inside.

Giron Escrima

Inside block to #7

McCune prepares to deliver a number 1 strike to Somera's left collarbone. Somera is in a ready position.

Somera steps to 1 o'clock with his right foot counter blocks McCune's weapon with an inside cross block Somera supports his asparagus knife with his left hand.

Somera leans forward and inserts his asparagus knife into McCune's right collarbone and slides his hand onto McCune's weapon hand.

Somera pulls out his weapon and chambers it to his right side, grabbing McCune's weapon wrist.

Somera finishes with a sonkete poke to McCune's mid section maintaining his grip on McCune's weapon wrist.

Outside block to #6

McCune prepares to deliver a number 2 strike to Somera's right collarbone. Somera is in a ready position.

Somera steps forward to 11 o'clock with his left foot, parry's McCune's weapon hand to the inside and counter block McCune's weapon using an asparagus knife.

Somera leans forward and sonkete pokes to McCune's right collarbone and parrying McCune's weapon hand to the inside.

Part 7: Twenty Styles of Grand Master Leo M. Giron

Somera pulls out his weapon and chambers to his right side, grabbing McCune's weapon wrist.

Somera finishes with a sonkete poke to McCune's mid section maintaining his left hand in a ready position.

Giron Escrima

Left hand downward parry to #7

McCune prepares to deliver a number 2 strike to Somera's right collarbone.

Somera steps to 11 o'clock with his right foot "C" check McCune's weapon hand and counter blocks with a cross block.

Somera parries down McCune's weapon hand with his left hand to clear Somera's body.

Part 7: Twenty Styles of Grand Master Leo M. Giron

Somera parry's McCune's weapon to his outside and inserts a sonkete poke to McCune's right collarbone.

Somera pulls out his weapon and chambers to his right side, grabbing McCune's weapon wrist.

Somera finishes with a sonkete poke to McCune's mid section maintaining his grip on McCune's weapon hand.

Giron Escrima

Down beat soft to #5

McCune prepares to deliver a number 3 strike to Somera's left hip.

Somera steps to 1 o'clock with his right foot squats down faces the oncoming weapon and counter blocks with an inside block to McCune's weapon.

Somera parries down McCune's weapon by pushing down and rotating on the balls of Somera's feet, left hand in a ready position.

Part 7: Twenty Styles of Grand Master Leo M. Giron

Somera checks McCune's weapon arm and prepares his asparagus knife in a ready position to poke.

Somera leans forward and sonkete pokes McCune in his mid section maintaining his left hand check.

Giron Escrima

Deflection Back of Bolo left hand parry to #5

McCune prepares to deliver a number 3 strike to Somera's left hip.

Somera left hand parry's McCune's weapon hand, Somera step to 2 o'clock with his right foot and preparing to sonkete poke with his weapon to McCune's mid section.

Somera clears McCune's weapon to the inside and inserts a sonkete poke to McCune's mid section.

Part 7: Twenty Styles of Grand Master Leo M. Giron

Down beat hard to #5

1 McCune prepares to deliver a number 4 strike to Somera's right hip.

2 Somera prepares to left hand check and down beat deflection to McCune's strike.

3 Somera steps to 1 o'clock with his left foot, down beat deflects and left hand checks McCune while counter striking with a sonkete poke to McCune's mid section.

4 Somera drives a sonkete poke to the mid section of McCune and "C" checks McCune's weapon hand.

Deflect back of bolo

McCune delivers a number 4 strike to Somera's right hip; Somera anticipates and deflects the top of McCune's weapon.

Somera deflects down to McCune's weapon, Somera using the back of his asparagus knife.

Somera clears McCune's weapon with his left hand, steps to 1 o'clock with his right foot, inserts a sonkete poke to McCune's mid section.

#5 against #5

McCune prepares to deliver a number 5 strike to Somera's mid section.

Somera evades to 1 o'clock with his right foot, inside left hand parries to McCune's weapon using the flat side of his palm and inside deflects on coming weapon.

Somera inserts a sonkete poke to McCune's mid section, caution do not grab the blade, use the flat side of your palm to parry out weapon.

Deflection soft to #5

McCune prepares to deliver a number 5 strike to Somera's mid section.

Somera steps to 1 o'clock with his left foot and outside deflect McCune's weapon.

Somera clears McCune's weapon arm to the inside and inserts a sonkete poke to McCune's mid section.

6
Estilo Retirada

Right foot retreat follow hit

McCune prepares to deliver a number 1 strike to Somera's left collarbone.

Somera retreats with his right foot to 5 o'clock striking McCune's right outside wrist.

Left foot retreat follow hit

1

McCune prepares to deliver a number 2 strike to Somera's right collarbone.

2

Somera retreats with his left foot to 7 o'clock and strikes to the inside wrist of McCune.

Giron Escrima

Left wide foot retreat follow hit

McCune prepares to deliver a number 3 strike to Somera's left hip.

Somera, retreats wide with his left foot to 9 o'clock striking McCune to the outside weapon arm.

Right wide foot retreat follow hit

1 McCune prepares to deliver a number 4 strike to Somera's right hip.

2 Somera retreats wide with his left foot to 9 o'clock striking McCune to the inside weapon arm.

Left foot retreat follow hit

McCune prepares to deliver a number 5 strike to Somera's mid section.

Somera retreats with his left foot to 7 o'clock striking McCune to his inside weapon arm.

7
Estilo Elastico

Giron Escrima

Right foot lead, lean back follow hit

McCune prepares to deliver a number 1 strike to Somera's left collarbone; Somera leans forward to bait McCune.

As McCune strikes, Somera stretches back with his left foot to 7 o'clock and strikes upward to McCune's weapon hand.

Somera returns his counter strike to the back of McCune's arm and stretches forward not allowing McCune to escape.

Right foot lead, lean back against hit

1
McCune prepares to deliver a number 2 strike to Somera's right collarbone; Somera leans forward to bait McCune.

2
Somera retreats with his left foot to 7 o'clock stretching back striking McCune to his inside weapon arm.

3
Somera returns his counter strike to the back of McCune's arm and stretches forward not allowing McCune to escape applying a left hand check.

Giron Escrima

Right foot lead, lean back inside hit and return

McCune prepares to deliver a number 3 strike to Somera's left hip; Somera leans forward to bait McCune.

McCune prepares to deliver a number 3 strike to Somera's left hip; Somera leans forward to bait McCune.

Somera returns his counter strike to the back of McCune's shoulder and stretches forward not allowing McCune to escape, notice the reach and weapon position.

Right foot lead, lean back hit against and return

1
McCune prepares to deliver a number 4 strike to Somera's right hip; Somera leans forward to bait McCune.

2
Somera stretches forward right foot to 1 o'clock and delivers a direct strike to the back of McCune's arm.

3
Somera stretches back evading McCune's strike chambering his weapon to his left side.

4
Somera finishes McCune by stretching forward not allowing McCune to escape striking McCune to the back of his weapon hand.

Right foot lead, lean back inside hit

As McCune delivers a number 5 to Somera's mid section, Somera stretches backwards with his left foot to 6 o'clock striking McCune to the inside of his weapon hand.

Somera returns his counter strike to the back of McCune's shoulder and stretches forward not allowing McCune to escape, notice the reach and weapon position.

8
Fondo Fuerte

Direct hit

Somera in a ready position with his back to the wall, McCune prepares to deliver a number 1 to Somera's left collarbone.

Somera evades left with left foot to 9 o'clock striking McCune to the inside of his weapon hand.

Somera advances forward with his foot to 1 o'clock "C" checking McCune's weapon hand Somera chambering his weapon to his right side.

Somera will finish by counter striking to McCune's weapon hand.

Back of bolo hit to throat

1 Somera in a ready position with is back to the wall, McCune prepares to deliver a number 2 to Somera right collarbone.

2 Somera sweep blocks McCune's strike.

3 Somera counter strikes directly to McCune's throat.

4 Somera returns an upward counter strike to the outside of McCune's weapon hand along with a left hand check.

Giron Escrima

Right foot wide lead inside block

Somera in a ready position, McCune prepares to deliver a number 3 strike to the left hip.

Somera steps to 3 o'clock with his right foot, left hand checks and inside counter blocks using the flat side of Somera's blade to McCune's weapon hand.

Somera counter strikes directly to the mid section and grabs McCune's weapon wrist.

Part 7: Twenty Styles of Grand Master Leo M. Giron

Somera follows up with an upward strike to McCune's mid section maintaining his left hand grip.

Somera prepares to sonkete poke McCune's head.

Giron Escrima

Left foot lead to X block

McCune prepares to deliver a number 4 strike to Somera's right hip.

Somera with his back to the wall counter blocks McCune's strike with the flat side of his blade and checks McCune with his left hand.

Somera maintains his left foot wide lead to 9 o'clock, counter strikes McCune's weapon hand and inserts a sonkete poke to McCune's mid section keeping his left hand check on McCune's weapon wrist.

Right foot lead deflection

1 McCune prepares to deliver a number 5 strike to Somera's mid section.

2 Somera with his back to the wall counter blocks McCune's strike with the flat side of his blade and steps wide with his right foot to 9 o'clock.

3 Somera parry's McCune's weapon to the outside of Somera's body using the flat side of his blade.

4 Somera steps with his left foot to 11 o'clock "C" checks McCune's weapon forearm and strikes McCune to his mid section.

9
Contra Compas

Roof block

1

McCune prepares to deliver a number 1 strike to Somera's left collarbone.

2

Somera steps to 1 o'clock with his right foot and counter block McCune's weapon with a roof block using the flat side of Somera's weapon, Somera left hand checks McCune's weapon hand.

3

Somera-contra compas snap hits McCune to the face before chambering his weapon using the tip of his blade.

Giron Escrima

Left hand parry

McCune prepares to deliver a number 2 strike to Somera's right collarbone.

Somera steps to 1 o'clock with his right foot, direct checks McCune's weapon hand and contra compas snap hits McCune to the head before chambering Somera's weapon.

Somera-contra compas snap hits McCune to the head using the tip of his blade.

Left hand check

1. McCune prepares to deliver a number 3 strike to Somera's left hip.

2. Somera left hand checks McCune's weapon hand and contra compas snap hits McCune's weapon arm.

3. Somera steps to 1 o'clock with his left foot and parry's out McCune's weapon arm to his right side, Somera chambers his weapon to his right side.

4. Somera counter strikes to McCune's weapon forearm.

Left foot lead sweep block

McCune prepares to deliver a number 4 strike to Somera's right hip.

Somera steps to 11 o'clock with his left foot checks McCune's weapon forearm and contra compas snap hits McCune's weapon hand.

Somera will finish his contra compas striking to McCune's forearm.

Part 7: Twenty Styles of Grand Master Leo M. Giron

Outside to #1 evade

1

McCune prepares to deliver a number 5 strike to Somera's mid section.

2

Somera evades and steps to 11 o'clock with this left foot, outside counter blocks with the flat side of his blade

3

Somera runs his blade up McCune's weapon and contra compas snap hits McCune's weapon hand.

10
Estilo Redonda

Inside Horizontal

McCune prepares to deliver a number 1 strike to Somera's left collarbone.

Somera steps to 12 o'clock with his right foot and begin his redonda counter strike circling his weapon over his head to generate striking power.

Somera redonda strikes to the inside of McCune's weapon hand.

Giron Escrima

Outside forward figure 8

1. McCune prepares to deliver a number 2 strike to Somera's right collarbone.

2. Somera steps to 12 o'clock with his right foot and prepares his forward redonda strike.

3. Somera starts his redonda strike to McCune's weapon hand using the tip of his blade.

4. Somera follows through with his redonda strike to McCune's weapon hand.

Hit against

1 McCune prepares to deliver a number 3 strike to Somera's left hip.

2 Somera steps to 12 o'clock with his right foot and begin his redonda counter strike circling his weapon over his head to generate striking power.

3 Somera redonda strikes to the inside of McCune's weapon hand.

Giron Escrima

Horizontal follow hit to forearm to ankle

McCune prepares to deliver a number 4 strike to Somera's right hip.

Somera steps to 12 o'clock with his right foot and begin his redonda counter strike circling his weapon to the inside of McCune's strike.

Somera steps to 12 o'clock with his right foot and begin his redonda counter strike circling his weapon to the inside of McCune's strike.

Part 7: Twenty Styles of Grand Master Leo M. Giron

4

Somera follows through with his redonda strike circling his weapon over his head to generate striking power.

5

Somera finishes his redonda strike to inside of McCune's inside ankle.

Outside upward figure 8 and return

McCune prepares to deliver a number 5 strike to Somera's mid section.

Somera steps wide to 9 o'clock with his left foot and outside redonda strikes to McCune's outside forearm.

Somera follows through with his redonda counter strike circling his weapon to the side of Somera's body to generate striking power.

Part 7: Twenty Styles of Grand Master Leo M. Giron

Somera continues his upward redonda circle strike and prepares to strike McCune's weapon arm.

Somera finishes his upward redonda strike to McCune's weapon arm.

11
Combate Adentro

Left hand parry against

1
McCune prepares to deliver a number 1 strike to Somera's left collarbone.

2
Somera steps to 10 o'clock with his left foot, left hand parry's to the outside of McCune's weapon hand and slices through McCune's weapon forearm.

3
Somera follows through with is slice and left hand parry's McCune's weapon hand to the right side of Somera's body.

4
Somera finishes his combate adentro strike to the outside of McCune's weapon forearm.

Left hand parry against bolo and dagger

McCune prepares to deliver a number 2 strike to Somera's right collarbone.

Somera ducks under McCune's strike and steps to 2 o'clock with his right foot Somera inside left hand parry's McCune's weapon hand and slices against to McCune's weapon forearm.

Part 7: Twenty Styles of Grand Master Leo M. Giron

McCune delivers a left hand dagger strike to Somera mid section Somera prepares to combat adentro strike against McCune's dagger hand.

Somera outside left hand parry's McCune's dagger hand and combate adentro strikes against.

Giron Escrima

Left hand parry against to dagger arm

McCune prepares to deliver a number 3 strike to Somera's left hip.

Somera steps wide with his left foot to 9 o'clock and "C" checks McCune's dagger hand.

Somera parry's through McCune's dagger hand with this left hand and slices through McCune's dagger forearm with his weapon.

Part 7: Twenty Styles of Grand Master Leo M. Giron

McCune delivers a number 3 with his right weapon to Somera's left hip, Somera parry's down McCune's weapon hand and prepares to combate adentro strike.

Somera-combate adentro slices through McCune's right weapon hand with his weapon.

Giron Escrima

Left hand parry to bolo arm

McCune prepares to deliver a number 4 strike to Somera's right hip.

Somera steps to 2 o'clock with his right foot, left hand parry downward and slices McCune's right weapon hand.

Part 7: Twenty Styles of Grand Master Leo M. Giron

3
McCune delivers a number 4 strike with his left hand dagger to Somera's right hip.

4
Somera parry's through McCune's dagger hand with this left hand and slices through McCune's dagger forearm.

Left hand parry outside hit to dagger arm

McCune prepares to deliver a number 5 strike with his right bolo knife and left hand dagger to Somera's mid section.

Somera left hand parry's McCune's left dagger hand and outside slices McCune's left forearm.

Somera step's to 9 o'clock with his left foot and left hand parry's McCune's left dagger hand slices inside McCune's left forearm.

Part 7: Twenty Styles of Grand Master Leo M. Giron

4

McCune prepares to deliver a number 5 with his right bolo knife to Somera's mid section.

5

Somera outside left hand parry's McCune's right bolo knife hand and slices to the inside of McCune's right bolo knife forearm.

6

Somera slice through McCune's right bolo knife forearm and finish with a strike to McCune's right shoulder.

12
Estilo Macabebe

Shoulder block

1. McCune prepares to deliver a number 2 strike to Somera's right collarbone.

2. Somera steps to 10 o'clock with his left foot and should blocks McCune's strike blocking McCune's strike in the cradle of the block. Somera's left weapon pointing up, right weapon pointing down.

3. Somera sweeps back his left weapon and strikes McCune's forearm with his right weapon.

4. Somera finishes with multiple weaving (sinawali) strikes with bother weapons to McCune's body and weapon hand.

Roof block

McCune prepares to deliver a number 1 strike to Somera's left collarbone.

Somera steps to 1 o'clock with his right foot and roof blocks McCune's strike blocking McCune's strike in the cradle of the block. Somera endeavors to keep his two sticks together to make a strong block with both weapons.

Somera pushes out with this left weapon to the outside of his body and prepares to strike with his right weapon.

Part 7: Twenty Styles of Grand Master Leo M. Giron

4

Somera strikes McCune with his right weapon maintaining pressure on McCune's striking weapon.

5

Somera finishes with multiple weaving (sinawali) strikes with both weapons to McCune's body and weapon hand.

Switch

1 McCune prepares to deliver a number 3 strike to Somera's left hip.

2 Somera steps to 12 o'clock with this right foot and switch blocks McCune's strike blocking McCune's strike in the cradle of his block. Somera's right weapon pointing down left weapon pointing up.

3 Somera parry's down and out McCune's weapon with his left weapon Somera's right weapon rotates to the outside of McCune's right weapon arm.

4 Somera strikes with his right weapon to the outside of McCune's right weapon arm. Somera chambers his left weapon to his right side.

Part 7: Twenty Styles of Grand Master Leo M. Giron

5

Somera strikes with his left weapon to McCune's right weapon arm and chambers his right weapon to Somera's right side.

6

Somera strikes with his right weapon to McCune's right weapon hand and chambers his left weapon to Somera's right side.

7

Somera finishes his weaving (sinawali) strikes to McCune's right weapon arm.

X block

McCune prepares to deliver a number 4 strike to Somera's right hip.

Somera step's to 1 o'clock with his right foot placing McCune's strike in the cradle of Somera's "X" block left weapon pointing up right weapon pointing down.

Somera parries down McCune's weapon with his left weapon to clear Somera's body.

Part 7: Twenty Styles of Grand Master Leo M. Giron

4

Somera clears McCune's weapon Somera chambers his right weapon on his right side.

5

Somera counter strikes McCune's right inside forearm with his right weapon and chambers his left weapon to his left side.

6

Somera will finish with weaving (sinawali) strikes to McCune's body.

Giron Escrima

Cane X block

1 McCune prepares to deliver a number 5 strike to Somera's mid section. Somera's right weapon pointing down using it as a walking cane and left weapon pointing up.

2 Somera step's to 1 o'clock evades McCune's strike, Somera catches McCune's strike in the cradle of his two weapons, right weapon pointing down left weapon pointing up.

3 Somera's right weapon hooks McCune's right wrist and rakes McCune's eyes, his left weapon maintains pressure on McCune's weapon.

Part 7: Twenty Styles of Grand Master Leo M. Giron

Somera pulls back his right weapon to his right side and strikes McCune's with his left weapon to McCune's arm.

Somera stretches forward to strike McCune with his right weapon.

Somera strikes McCune to his groin Somera chambers his left weapon to his left side preparing to finish McCune with weaving (sinawali) strikes.

Giron Escrima

Disarm stick pointing up

McCune prepares to deliver a number 1 strike to Somera's left collarbone.

Somera steps to 1 o'clock with his right foot and roof blocks McCune's strike placing his strike in the cradle of the block.

Somera applies pressure to McCune's right weapon with his left weapon and strikes McCune with his right weapon to McCune's right weapon inside forearm.

Part 7: Twenty Styles of Grand Master Leo M. Giron

4

Somera strikes through with his right weapon and strikes the back of McCune's right thumb using the back of Somera's weapon.

5

Somera steps to 10 o'clock with his left foot pulls with his right weapon to Somera right side and strikes McCune with his left weapon to the back of McCune's arm.

Giron Escrima

Disarm should hook

1
McCune prepares to deliver a number 2 strike to Somera's right collarbone.

2
Somera steps to 10 o'clock with his left foot and prepares a shoulder block against McCune's strike.

3
Somera right weapon keeps pressure on McCune's weapon Somera's left weapons slides to the inside and strikes McCune's right thumb.

4
Somera inserts his left weapon and hooks McCune's right wrist rotating Somera's weapon with his palm turning down, Somera chambers his weapon to his right side.

Part 7: Twenty Styles of Grand Master Leo M. Giron

5
Somera continues his rotating with his left weapon Somera's using the hilt of his right weapon to lock his left weapon and strikes McCune's head.

6
Somera's pulls his left weapon and the force from his right weapon strike disarms McCune.

7
Somera delivers his finishing weaving (sinawali) strikes to McCune's body.

Disarm switch stick pointing up

McCune prepares to deliver a number 3 strike to Somera's left hip.

Somera steps to 12 o'clock blocks McCune's strike placing McCune's strike in the cradle of Somera's block.

Somera's right weapon slides up and to the outside of McCune's weapon striking McCune's weapon hand, Somera's left weapon maintains pressure on the inside tip of McCune's weapon.

Part 7: Twenty Styles of Grand Master Leo M. Giron

4

Somera pushing with his left weapon towards McCune, Somera's right weapon is pulled back to Somera's right side.

5

Somera strikes McCune's arm with his left weapon and chambers his right weapon to his right side disarming McCune's weapon.

6

Somera follows up with weaving (sinawali) strikes to McCune's right arm.

Disarm X block to hook

McCune prepares to deliver a number 4 strike to Somera's right hip.

Somera steps to 1 o'clock with his right foot and prepares to block McCune's strike Somera's left weapon pointing up and right weapon pointing down.

Somera blocks McCune's strike by catching McCune's strike in the cradle of Somera's block.

Part 7: Twenty Styles of Grand Master Leo M. Giron

Somera inserts his left weapon to the inside of McCune's weapon hand striking McCune's thumb, Somera maintains pressure on McCune's weapon with his right weapon.

Somera rotates his left weapon clockwise locking McCune's weapon, Somera chambers his right weapon to his right side.

Somera locks his right hit weapon between McCune's thumb and Somera left weapon and delivers a strike to McCune's head with his right weapon.

Giron Escrima

7

Somera disarms McCune's weapon hand by pulling his left weapon back towards Somera's body and following through with his right hand strike to McCune's head.

8

Somera chambers back his left weapon under his right weapon arm.

9

Somera completes his disarm by following up with weaving (sinawali) strikes to McCune's body.

Disarm X block Cane

1

McCune prepares to deliver a number 5 strike to Somera's mid section. Somera's right weapon pointing down using it as a walking cane and left weapon pointing up.

2

Somera steps to 1 o'clock evades McCune's strike Somera catches McCune's strike in the cradle of his two weapons.

3

Somera's right weapon hooks McCune's right wrist and rakes McCune's eyes his left weapon maintains pressure on McCune's weapon.

Giron Escrima

4

Somera pulls back his right weapon to his right side and strikes McCune's with his left weapon to McCune's arm.

5

Somera follows up with right hand reverse weapon and left forward hand weaving (sinawali) strikes to McCune's body.

13
Tero Pisada

Giron Escrima

Hit against to weapon

1 McCune prepares to deliver a number 1 strike to Somera's left collarbone.

2 Somera steps to 2 o'clock with his right foot and chambers his weapon to his right side.

3 Somera with paralyzing force strikes the end of McCune's weapon using dos manos (two hands) Somera's left hand over his right-handed grip.

4 Somera follows though with his strike paralyzing McCune's weapon hand.

Part 7: Twenty Styles of Grand Master Leo M. Giron

5

Somera chambers his weapon to his left side to counter strike McCune.

6

Somera strikes to McCune's body.

7

Somera finishes his strike to McCune's head using dos manos (two hand) strike.

Giron Escrima

Hit against to weapon

McCune prepares to deliver a number 2 strike to Somera's right collarbone.

Somera steps wide to 9 o'clock with his left foot and chambers the weapon to his left side.

Somera with paralyzing force strikes the end of McCune's weapon using dos manos (two hands) Somera's left hand over his right-handed grip.

Part 7: Twenty Styles of Grand Master Leo M. Giron

Somera follows though with his strike.

Somera chambers his weapon to his left side and steps with his right foot to 2 o'clock.

Somera finishes McCune with dos manos (two hands) strike to McCune's head.

Giron Escrima

Inside hit against down

McCune prepares to deliver a number 3 strike to Somera's left hip.

Somera steps wide to 3 o'clock with his right foot and chambers the weapon to his right side.

Somera with paralyzing force strikes the end of McCune's weapon using dos manos (two hands) Somera's left hand over his right-handed grip.

Part 7: Twenty Styles of Grand Master Leo M. Giron

Somera follows though with his strike steps forward with his left foot and chambers his weapon to his left side.

Somera steps to 1 o'clock with his right foot and finish his strike to McCune's head.

Giron Escrima

Outside hit against down

1 McCune prepares to deliver a number 4 strike to Somera's right hip. Somera anticipates and steps to 9 o'clock with his left foot.

2 Somera chambers his weapon to his left side to counter strike McCune and draws his right foot up to increase his striking force.

3 Somera with paralyzing force strikes the end of McCune's weapon using dos manos (two hands) Somera's left hand over his right-handed grip.

Part 7: Twenty Styles of Grand Master Leo M. Giron

4

Somera steps to 9 o'clock with his right foot and chambers his weapon to his right side.

5

Somera finishes McCune with dos manos (two hands) strike to McCune's head.

Giron Escrima

Outside hit against down

McCune prepares to deliver a number 5 strike to Somera's mid section. Somera anticipates and steps to 9 o'clock with his left foot.

Somera chambers his weapons to his left side to counter strike McCune.

Somera chambers his weapons to his left side to counter strike McCune and draws his right foot up to increase his striking force.

Part 7: Twenty Styles of Grand Master Leo M. Giron

4 Somera with paralyzing force strikes the end of McCune's weapon using dos manos (two hands) Somera's left hand over his right-handed grip.

5 Somera steps to 3 o'clock with his right foot and finish his strike to McCune's head.

14
Media Media

Left hand parry to Media Media snap hits

Herrera (bolo girl) prepares to deliver a number 1 strike to Somera's left collarbone.

Somera steps to 11 o'clock with his left foot, chambers his weapon to his right side and parry's the outside of Herrera's weapon hand.

Somera will strike Herrera's head while maintain his left hand parry.

Giron Escrima

Left hand check to Media Media snap hits

Herrera prepares to deliver a number 2 strike to Somera's right collarbone.

Somera steps to 11 o'clock with his left foot, chambers his weapon to his right side and parry's the outside of Herrera's weapon hand.

Somera will strike Herrera's head while maintain his left hand parry.

Left hand check to Media Media snap hits

1

Herrera prepares to deliver a number 3 strike to Somera's left hip.

2

Somera steps to 1 o'clock with his right foot, chambers his weapon to his right side and "C" checks Herrera's weapon hand.

3

Somera will strike Herrera's head while maintain his left hand check.

Left hand downward check to Media Media snap hits

Herrera prepares to deliver a number 4 strike to Somera's right hip.

Somera steps to 11 o'clock with his left foot, left hand parry's Herrera's weapon hand and clears the weapon to his left side Somera chambers his weapon to his right side.

Somera will strike Herrera's head while maintain his left hand check.

Inside evade Left hand check to Media Media snap hits

Herrera prepares to deliver a number 5 strike to Somera's mid section.

Somera evades to the inside of Herrera's strike and steps to 1 o'clock Somera will "C" check Herrera's weapon hand.

Somera will strike Herrera's head while maintain his left hand check.

15
Cadena de Mano

Part 7: Twenty Styles of Grand Master Leo M. Giron

Outside Left hand Parry

Herrera prepares to deliver a number 1 forward dagger strike to Somera's left collarbone (1). Somera steps to 1 o'clock with his left foot and outside left hand parry's Herrera's weapon hand (2). Somera grabs and parries down Herrera's dagger hand Somera pulls (3). Herrera's counters by pulling back her dagger, Somera applies a left hand thumb pressure to the back of Herrera's hand and also grabs with his right hand to Herrera's dagger hand (4). Somera applies with his two hands thumb pressure to the back of Herrera's dagger hand (5). Somera directs Herrera's dagger to cut Herrera's throat, Somera using his two hands (6).

Giron Escrima

Right hand check break hinge

1 Herrera prepares to deliver a number 2 forward dagger strike to Somera's right collarbone.

2 Somera steps to 10 o'clock with his left foot and checks against Herrera's dagger hand using his right hand.

3 Somera continues to rotate Herrera's dagger hand down twisting Herrera's dagger hand.

4 Somera rotates Herrera's dagger to the left side of Somera's body and starts to grab Herrera's dagger hand with his right hand.

Part 7: Twenty Styles of Grand Master Leo M. Giron

5 Somera grabs with both hands to Herrera's dagger hand and starts to apply a reverse wrist lock and thumb pressure to the back of Herrera's dagger hand.

6 Somera grabs to control Herrera's dagger hand with his left hand and strikes Herrera's back elbow with his right forearm.

7 Somera repositions both of his hand and grabs Herrera's weapon hand and starts to turn Herrera's dagger wrist towards her mid section.

8 With Herrera's own dagger Somera inserts Herrera's dagger into her mid section.

Giron Escrima

Left hand check under

Herrera prepares to deliver a number 3 forward dagger strike to Somera's left hip.

Somera steps wide to 10 o'clock with his right foot and strikes the inside of Herrera's weapon forearm with Somera's left forearm.

With Somera's right hand he inserts it to the outside of Herrera's weapon hand.

Part 7: Twenty Styles of Grand Master Leo M. Giron

4

Somera locks Herrera's weapon hand with his left and right hands and rotates his hands in a counter clockwise direction, grabbing Herrera's weapon wrist.

5

Somera collapse Herrera's weapon hand wrist facing her dagger towards her.

6

Somera inserts Herrera's dagger into her throat.

Giron Escrima

Left hand check under break hinge

Herrera prepares to deliver a number 4 forward dagger strike to Somera's right hip.

Somera steps wide to 10 o'clock with his left foot and strikes the outside of Herrera's forearm with his right arm and inserts his left arm to the inside locking Herrera's weapon arm.

Somera locks Herrera's weapon hand with his left and right hands and rotates his hand in a clockwise direction, grabbing Herrera's weapon wrist.

Part 7: Twenty Styles of Grand Master Leo M. Giron

With both hands Somera collapse Herrera's weapon wrist and locks Herrera's weapon hand using thumb pressure to the back of Herrera's hand.

Somera grabs Herrera's inside elbow with his right hand and rotates Herrera's weapon hand towards Herrera's mid section.

Somera inserts Herrera's dagger into her mid section.

Inside Left hand check break hinge take down

Herrera prepares to deliver a number 5 forward dagger strike to Somera's mid section.

Somera steps to 1 o'clock with his right foot and prepares to grab Herrera's inside weapon hand.

Somera strikes Herrera with an open palm strike to her weapon elbow and maintains his left hand grab on Herrera's weapon hand.

Somera pulls Herrera's elbow with his right hand and rotates her weapon hand counter clockwise.

Part 7: Twenty Styles of Grand Master Leo M. Giron

5

Somera continues the rotation of Herrera's weapon hand and Somera inserts his right arm under Herrera's elbow and grabs Herrera's throat.

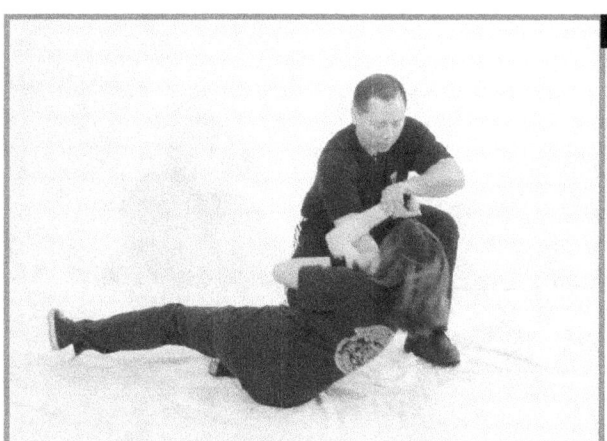

6

Somera pulls Herrera's weapon hand down with his left hand and pushes Herrera's throat down with his right hand.

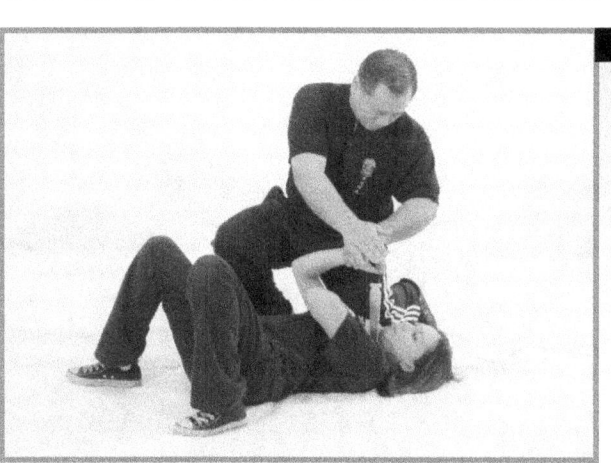

7

Somera pulls his right hand off of Herrera's throat and repositions his right hand over his left hand and strikes down inserting Herrera's own weapon into her throat.

Giron Escrima

Left hand parry break hinge take down

McCune prepares to deliver a number 1 punch to Somera's left collarbone, Somera in a ready position.

Somera left foot is at 11 o'clock and outside parry's McCune's punch with his left hand.

Somera left hand grabs McCune's right hand rotating it clockwise, Somera right hand grabs McCune's inside right elbow.

Part 7: Twenty Styles of Grand Master Leo M. Giron

Somera inserts his left arm to the inside of McCune's right arm his left hand will relocate on the top of McCune's shoulder, Somera's right hand will also relocate on the top of McCune's shoulder.

Somera pivots on his left foot and rotates his right foot clockwise dragging McCune to the ground.

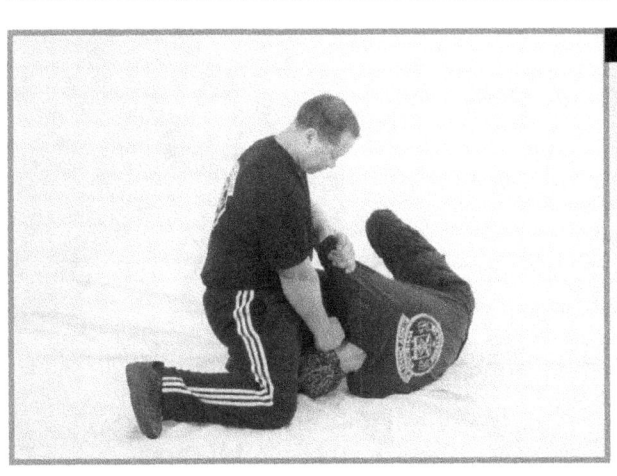

Somera drops his right knee to McCune's head and finish with a right hand punch to the back of McCune's neck keeping his left arm locked on McCune's right shoulder.

Giron Escrima

Left hand check elbow strike take down

McCune prepares to deliver a number 2 punch to Somera's right collarbone, Somera in a ready position.

McCune punches with his left hand, Somera will grab to the outside of McCune's punch with his left hand.

Somera steps to 12 o'clock with his right foot pulls McCune's left hand down and close to Somera body, Somera delivers a forearm strike to the back of McCune's left arm.

Part 7: Twenty Styles of Grand Master Leo M. Giron

4

Somera pulls McCune's left arm with his left hand down and pushes down the back of McCune's arm.

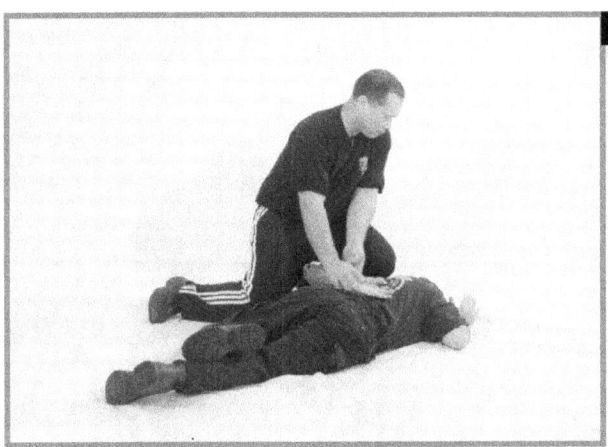

5

Somera put McCune down on the ground and repositions McCune's left arm behind McCune's back. Somera left knee strikes McCune's head and positions his right knee on McCune's back.

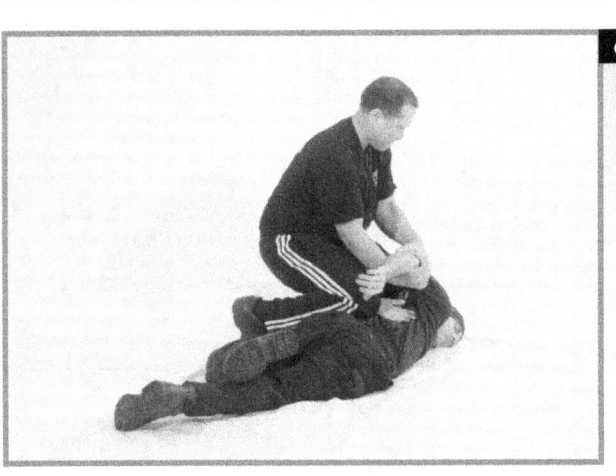

6

Somera left and right knees are repositions on McCune's back, Somera grabs McCune's right arm and pulls locking McCune's arms and shoulders.

Giron Escrima

Left hand strike shoulder lock take down

1 McCune prepares to deliver a right hand number 3 punch to Somera's left mid section, Somera in a ready position.

2 Somera steps to 10 o'clock with his left foot and strikes with his left arm to the inside of McCune's inside elbow.

3 Somera grabs the outside of McCune's right elbow with his right hand; Somera inserts his left forearm to McCune's inside right forearm.

4 Somera inserts his left hand to the top of McCune's right shoulder.

Part 7: Twenty Styles of Grand Master Leo M. Giron

5

Somera pulls McCune's shoulder down and strikes with his right knee to McCune's right shoulder.

6

Somera turns McCune's shoulders clockwise and maintains his grip with his left arm to McCune's right arm; Somera follows McCune to the ground.

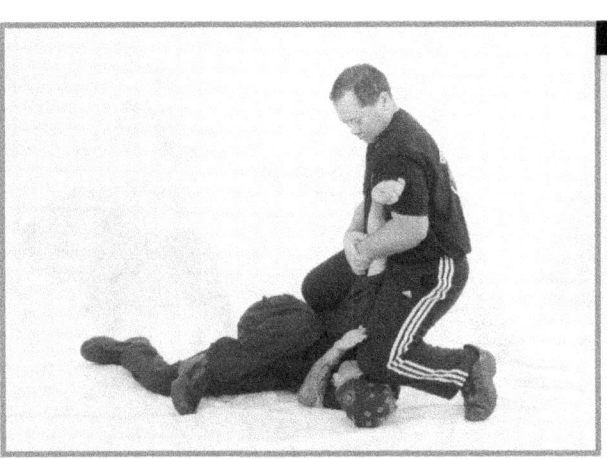

7

Somera left knee strikes to McCune's head and right knee strikes to McCune's right side ribs. Somera locks McCune's right arm against his body.

Left hand punch evade take down

McCune prepares to deliver a left hand number 4 punch to Somera's left mid section, Somera in a ready position.

Somera step with his right foot to 1 o'clock and evades McCune's punch. Somera grab s McCune's left hand with his left hand Somera follows up with a right outside forearm strike to McCune's outside left arm.

Somera pulls McCune's left hand and inserts his right hand to the inside of McCune's left arm.

Part 7: Twenty Styles of Grand Master Leo M. Giron

4

Somera places his right hand to the back of McCune's head and pulls with his left hand.

5

Somera pulls McCune down and rotates his head counter clockwise pulling McCune's left hand.

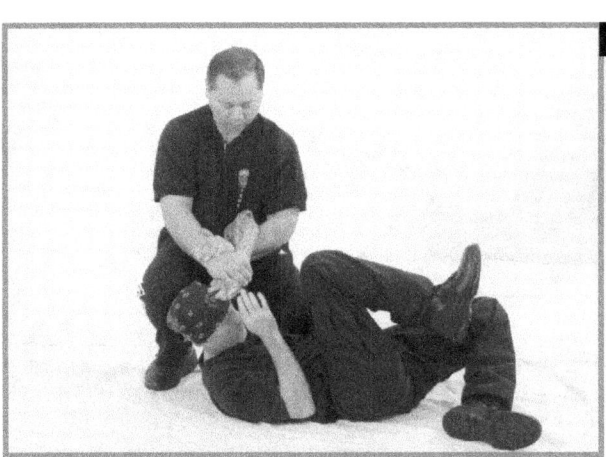

6

Somera inserts his left arm to the inside of McCune's inside arm and grabs his own right wrist. Somera finishes the lock with his right hand grab to McCune's left wrist. Somera knee strikes with his left knee to McCune's left ribs.

Giron Escrima

Evade right hand grab take down

McCune prepares to deliver a right hand number 5 punch to Somera's mid section, Somera in a ready position.

Somera steps to 11 o'clock with his left foot and grabs the top of McCune's right forearm.

Somera pulls McCune's right hand down and will left hand punch McCune's head and Somera then places his left thumb in McCune's right eye.

Part 7: Twenty Styles of Grand Master Leo M. Giron

Somera pulls McCune's right hand and compresses McCune's head down switch his left hand.

Somera pulls McCune down to the ground.

Somera knee strikes McCune's head with his left knee and places McCune's right elbow over his right thigh with his two hands pushes down.

Double strike left right hand parry Macabebe lock

1

McCune prepares to deliver a right hand number 1 punch and left hand number 2 punch to Somera's left and right collarbones, Somera in a ready position. This is Macabebe cadena de mano.

2

Somera's left foot to the 11 o'clock position and outside left hand parry's McCune's right punch.

3

Somera locates his left and right thumbs on the back of McCune's right hand and rotates McCune's right hand back in the diction of McCune.

4

Somera maintains his grip with his left hand on McCune's right hand, McCune punches with his left hand to Somera's right collarbone, Somera evades McCune's punch and outside parry's McCune's left elbow.

Part 7: Twenty Styles of Grand Master Leo M. Giron

Somera parry's McCune's left elbow to McCune's chest with his right hand and maintains his grip on McCune's left hand.

Somera parry's McCune's right arm counter clockwise into McCune's chest and parry's McCune's left arm in a counter clockwise motion.

Somera maintains his right hand grip on McCune's right wrist and locks McCune's left arm by parrying McCune's left arm behind Somera's right outside elbow, this will free Somera's left arm, Somera will punch McCune with his left hand to the face.

Double strike Left hand grab right hand parry Macabebe lock

1. McCune prepares to deliver a left hand number 2 punch and right hand number 1 punch to Somera's left and right collarbones, Somera in a ready position. This is Macabebe cadena de mano.

2. Somera left foot to 11 o'clock position and outside left hand parry's McCune's left punch.

3. Somera grabs McCune's left hand with his left hand and right elbow strike McCune's left bicep.

4. McCune counter punches with his right hand to Somera's head, Somera right hand parry's under McCune's punch.

Part 7: Twenty Styles of Grand Master Leo M. Giron

5

Somera maintains his left hand grip on McCune's left wrist and weaves his right arm clockwise around McCune's right and left arms.

6

Somera weaves his left arm to the outside of McCune's left forearm Somera's right hand is ready to grab and lock with his left forearm.

7

Somera Macabebe (weaving) locks to the both of McCune's arms, Somera locks McCune's arms and crushes McCune's elbows.

16
Escapo

Part 7: Twenty Styles of Grand Master Leo M. Giron

Left hand right hand parry

Herrera prepares to deliver a number 1 strike to Somera's left collarbone. Somera in a ready position (1). Somera steps to 10 o'clock and outside left hand parry's Herrera's weapon hand (2). Herrera prepares to deliver a number 9 strike to Somera's right ankle, Somera retreats his left foot to 8 o'clock (3). Somera outside right hand parry's Herrera's weapon hand down (4). Somera steps to 10 o'clock with his left foot, Herrera delivers a number 11 strike to Somera's left ankle and Somera inside left hand parry's Herrera's weapon hand to Somera's right side (5). Herrera returns a number 2 strike to Somera right collarbone, Somera retreats his left foot to 8 o'clock and prepares to parry under Herrera's strike (6).

Giron Escrima

Somera ducks under Herrera's strike and inside right hand parry's Herrera's weapon hand (7). Herrera returns a number 5 strike to Somera's mid section, Somera evades and steps to 10 o'clock with his left foot and preparing to left hand parry Herrera's right weapon hand (8). Somera parry's Herrera's number 5 strike and relocates his left and right handed thumbs to the back of Herrera's weapon hand (9). Herrera's try's to pull her right weapon hand away Somera will then collapse Herrera's right weapon wrist and slice her neck (10).

17
Estilo Bolante

Vertical block up and return strike

McCune prepares to deliver a number 1 strike to Somera's left collarbone. Somera in a ready position.

Somera steps to 11 o'clock with his left foot and uses the back of his stick to deflect McCune's weapon to Somera's right side.

Somera chambers his weapon to his right side.

Part 7: Twenty Styles of Grand Master Leo M. Giron

4

Somera counter strikes with a forward Bolante vertical strike to McCune's weapon arm.

5

Somera counter strikes with a forward vertical strike to McCune's head.

Giron Escrima

Vertical down direct hit

McCune prepares to deliver a number 2 strike to Somera's right collarbone. Somera in a ready position.

Somera steps to 11 o'clock with his left foot and chambers his weapon vertically to his right side.

Somera strikes McCune with a direct vertical Bolante strike to McCune's weapon forearm.

Part 7: Twenty Styles of Grand Master Leo M. Giron

Somera left hand "C" checks McCune's weapon forearm and chambers his weapon on his right side.

Somera strikes with an upward vertical Bolante strike to McCune's body.

Left hand parry vertical down and return

1 McCune prepares to deliver a number 3 strike to Somera's left hip. Somera in a ready position.

2 Somera steps back with his left foot to 6 o'clock and elastico (stretch) back and outside left hand parry's McCune's weapon and chambers his weapon vertically to his right side.

3 Somera strikes with a downward vertical Bolante strike to McCune's weapon forearm.

Part 7: Twenty Styles of Grand Master Leo M. Giron

4

Somera clears his weapon making sure he does not hit his weapon on the ground and prepares for McCune's counter strike.

5

Somera strikes with an upward vertical Bolante strike to McCune's body.

Left hand parry vertical strike down and return

McCune prepares to deliver a number 4 strike to Somera's right hip. Somera in a ready position.

Somera steps back with his left foot to 6 o'clock and elastico (stretch) back and outside left hand parry's McCune's weapon while chambering his weapon vertically to his right side.

Somera strikes with a downward vertical Bolante strike to McCune's body.

Part 7: Twenty Styles of Grand Master Leo M. Giron

Somera clears his weapon making sure he does not hit his weapon on the ground and with an upward Bolante strike hits McCune body.

Somera return strikes with a downward vertical Bolante strike to McCune's body.

Giron Escrima

Evade Left hand parry vertical downward strike and return

1 McCune prepares to deliver a number 5 strike to Somera's mid section. Somera in a ready position.

2 Somera steps to 11 o'clock with his left foot and chambers his weapon vertically to his right side and will outside left hand parry McCune's weapon hand.

3 Somera strikes McCune with a direct vertical Bolante strike to McCune's weapon forearm.

4 Somera clears his weapon making sure he does not hit his weapon on the ground and prepares for McCune's Bolante counter strike.

Part 7: Twenty Styles of Grand Master Leo M. Giron

5

Somera strikes with an upward vertical Bolante strike to McCune's weapon hand.

6

Somera vertically chambers his weapon to his right side.

7

Somera return his strikes with a downward vertical Bolante strike to McCune's weapon hand.

18
Tero Grave

Outside to Throat

1 McCune prepares to deliver a number 1 strike to Somera's left collarbone. Somera in a ready position.

2 Somera steps wide to 9 o'clock with his left foot and blocks to the outside of McCune's weapon using the flat side of Somera's blade.

3 Somera rotates his weapon towards McCune's throat.

4 Somera delivers a Tero Grave strike to McCune's throat.

Giron Escrima

Outside to eye

McCune prepares to deliver a number 2 strike to Somera's right collarbone. Somera in a ready position.

Somera steps to 11 o'clock with his left foot and counter blocks McCune's strike with a horizontal block with his weapon pointing in the direction of McCune's face, Somera also left hand "C" check McCune's weapon hand.

Somera delivers a Tero Grave strike to McCune's left eye.

Hit to temples

1 McCune prepares to deliver a number 3 strike to Somera's left hip. Somera in a ready position.

2 Somera left hand inside "C" checks McCune's weapon hand, Somera delivers a Tero Grave strike using the end of his weapon to the right temple.

3 Somera rotates his weapon to strike McCune's left temple and will maintain his left hand grab on McCune's weapon hand.

4 Somera delivers a Tero Grave strike to McCune's left temple.

Giron Escrima

Hit to throat

McCune prepares to deliver a number 4 strike to Somera's right hip. Somera in a ready position.

Somera steps wide to 9 o'clock with his left foot and chambers his weapon to his right side.

Somera delivers a Tero Grave strike to McCune's left ear using the tip of his weapon.

Hit Back of Head (medulla oblongata)

1

McCune prepares to deliver a number 5 strike to Somera's mid section. Somera in a ready position.

2

Somea steps out wide to 9 o'clock with his left foot and strikes McCune to the outside of McCune's weapon forearm, Somera strikes with the tip of his weapon.

3

Somera checks McCune's right shoulder with his left hand and chambers his weapon to his right side.

Giron Escrima

Somera strikes McCune to the top of his right shoulder.

Somera delivers his finishing Tero Grave strike to the back of McCune's neck (medulla oblongata).

19
Miscla (Mezcla) Contras

Multiple attacks

1

McCune and Herrera start their attack McCune prepares to deliver a number 1 strike to Somera's left collarbone. Somera in a ready position.

2

Somera position his body against and next to the wall so that the McCune and Herrera must come from one direction, Somera counter strikes to the inside of McCune's weapon forearm.

3

Somera forces McCune to the inside of Somera and follows through with his strike to McCune's forearm.

4

Somera disables McCune and McCune falls to the wayside were the rest of Somera group will finish off McCune; Somera prepares for Herrera the next attacker.

Part 7: Twenty Styles of Grand Master Leo M. Giron

5
Somera steps to 2 o'clock with this right foot and ducks under Herrera's strike to his head, Somera counter strikes Herrera with a follow inside strike cutting Herrera's inside forearm.

6
Somera advances forward and grabs the inside of Herrera's weapon hand with his left hand which forces Herrera to the outside of Somera as he advances forward to meet the next oncoming enemy.

7
Somera strikes Herrera with a backhand slice to Herrera's mid section and pushes her over with his left hand as he advances.

8
Somera advances forward to meet the next oncoming enemy while the rest of Somera's group will finish off McCune and Herrera.

20
Larga Mano

Left foot retreat direct upward hit

McCune prepares to deliver a number 1 strike to Somera's left collarbone. Somera is in a ready position (1). Somera retreats back to 8 o'clock with his left foot and strikes upward using the tip of his blade and striking McCune on the inside of McCune's weapon wrist (2). Somera stretches forward to strike McCune's outside weapon wrist (3). Somera stretches forward and strikes the outside of McCune's weapon wrist (4). Somera clears his weapon not to hit or damage his weapon on the ground (5). Somera stretches backwards and strikes upwards using the tip of his blade and striking McCune on the inside of McCune's weapon wrist (6).

Giron Escrima

Left foot retreat direct downward hit

McCune prepares to deliver a number 2 strike to Somera's right collarbone. Somera in a ready position.

Somera stretches forward with his right foot to 12 o'clock and strikes the outside of McCune's weapon forearm with the time of his blade.

Somera clears his weapon not to hit or damage his weapon on the ground.

Part 7: Twenty Styles of Grand Master Leo M. Giron

Somera stretches backwards and strikes upwards using the tip of his blade and striking McCune on the inside of McCune's weapon wrist.

Somera chambers his weapon on his left side and catches the back of his weapon with his open left palm ready to throw his weapon back at McCune to strike him.

Somera stretches forward to strike McCune's outside weapon wrist.

Giron Escrima

Long reaching wide hit against

McCune prepares to deliver a number 3 strike to Somera's left hip. Somera in a ready position.

Somera steps wide to 9 o'clock with his left foot and direct strikes to the inside of McCune's weapon hand using the tip of Somera's blade.

Part 7: Twenty Styles of Grand Master Leo M. Giron

McCune attempts to return a backhand strike but Somera advances forward with his right foot to 12 o'clock and meets McCune's outside wrist with the tip of his blade.

McCune strikes at Somera with a backhand strike to Somera's right hip but Somera strikes McCune with an inside follow strike using the tip of his blade.

Giron Escrima

Left foot wide follow hit and return

1 McCune prepares to deliver a number 4 strike to Somera's right hip. Somera in a ready position.

2 Somera steps to 9 o'clock with his left foot and strikes McCune with an inside follow hit using the tip of his blade.

3 Somera chambers his weapon to his left side and steps to 12 o'clock with his right foot.

4 Somera strikes down with a bartical strike to McCune's right collarbone.

Part 7: Twenty Styles of Grand Master Leo M. Giron

5

Somera clears his weapon not to hit or damage his weapon on the ground.

6

Somera returns an upward strike to the inside of McCune's right thigh using the tip of his blade.

7

Somera stretches forward and finishes McCune with a downward strike to McCune's right shoulder.

Giron Escrima

Advance direct hit

McCune prepares to deliver a number 5 strike to Somera's mid section. Somera is in a ready position.

Somera steps out wide to 9 o'clock with this left foot and counter strikes with an upward strike to the back of McCune's elbow.

Somera advances forward with his right foot to 12 o'clock and "C" checks the back of McCune's shoulder and will chamber his weapon to his right side not allow his weapon to go pass the tip of McCune's weapon.

Part 7: Twenty Styles of Grand Master Leo M. Giron

4 Somera will take a wide step with his left foot to 9 o'clock and prepare to strike McCune's weapon shoulder.

5 Somera strikes McCune to the top of his weapon shoulder and prepares his final blow to McCune's back of his head.

6 Somera delivers his finishing strike stretching towards McCune and strikes to the back of McCune's neck with both hands (dos manos).

Lineage of Giron Arnis Escriama
Bahala Na Martial Arts Association

Leo M. Giron
Grand Master Emeritus
Founder Bahala Na Martial Arts

Antonio E. Somera
Grand Master

Kirk McCune
Master

Joel Juanitas
Master

Instructors

Terry Joven	Dan Inosanto	David Dizon	David Hines	Michael Giron
	Lawrence Motta	Roy Atay	Phil Matedne	Gene Inis
David Alessandro	Amelia DeAnzo	Jim Johnson	Dexter Labanog	Thorsten Meyer
	Duncan Geddes	Barry Shriear	Steve Tarani	Frank Buchner
Norman Galera		Victorino Ton Honorary	June Gotico	Jim Tabias
	Joe Pacpaco Honorary			

www.ingramcontent.com/pod-product-compliance
Lightning Source LLC
Chambersburg PA
CBHW081344080526

44588CB00016B/2376